A HISTORY OF
BETHEL PENTECOSTAL CHURCH
IN SARNIA, ONTARIO

A History of
Bethel Pentecostal Church
in Sarnia, Ontario

by

CALEB HOWARD COURTNEY

ISBN 978-0-9953299-0-4 (print)
ISBN 978-0-9953299-1-1 (pdf)

Published in heartfelt cooperation with Bethel Pentecostal Church
1565 London Line, Sarnia, Ontario, Canada N7T 7H2
www.bethelsarnia.com

Bethel Pentecostal Church is affiliated with the Pentecostal Assemblies of Canada.

Library and Archives Canada Cataloguing in Publication

Courtney, Caleb Howard, author
     A history of Bethel Pentecostal Church in Sarnia, Ontario / by Caleb
Howard Courtney.

Includes bibliographical references and index.
Issued in print and electronic formats.

ISBN 978-0-9953299-0-4 (paperback).
ISBN 978-0-9953299-1-1 (pdf).

     1. Bethel Pentecostal Church (Sarnia, Ont.)—History. 2. Pentecostal
Assemblies of Canada. 3. Pentecostal churches—Ontario—Sarnia—History.
4. Sarnia (Ont.)—Church history. I. Bethel Pentecostal Church (Sarnia,
Ont.), issuing body II. Title.

BX8762.A43O57 2016   289.9'40971327   C2016-906449-2
                                                    C2016-906450-6

Cover photo: Edna Riblet and her Sunday School Mission on White Street in Sarnia in the late 1930's.
Cover layout: Cayden Gibb, Sarnia, Ontario.
First printing in 2016 (800 copies) by Haines Frontier Printing Ltd., Sarnia, Ontario, established 1912.
Subsequent printings beginning in 2021 by Amazon.com or their affiliates.

Contents

Foreword vii

Acknowledgments ix

1. Introduction 1
2. Sarnia's First Pentecostal Missionary 4
3. The Earliest Pentecostal Churches in Sarnia 8
4. The White Street Mission & Edna Riblet 19
5. Bethel Pentecostal Church at 245 Essex Street 30
6. Bethel Pentecostal Church at 1565 London Line 39
7. The Sarnia Revival 50
8. Modern History (2007-2016) 54

Asides 63

Suggested Additional Reading 66

Addenda 68

    How Pentecost Came to Toronto (1907) 68

    Testimony of Barbara Johnston of Sarnia (1909) 72

    Evangelist Helps Save Sarnia Man from Drowning (1938) 76

    Sunday School in What is Known as Shanty Town – Sarnia (1939) 78

    Long-Time Organist Marks 60 Years (2016) 79

    Bethel Pentecostal Church Celebrates 80 Years (2016) 81

Lists of Pastors, Church Staff, and Board Members 83

Photo Credits 89

Notes 91

Selected Bibliography 101

Index 108

Foreword

In the busyness of ministry life, we almost missed a significant anniversary of Bethel Pentecostal Church—80 years of continuous ministry presence in Sarnia, Ontario. It was Caleb Courtney that alerted me to this fact. Realizing the importance of this event, I quickly asked him if he would be willing to write an article for our monthly Connect church bulletin. "Just 4 pages," I said, "… of our history … with photos." Caleb replied that he was very busy with finishing his Master's Degree in Theological Studies at Tyndale Seminary in Toronto and did not think he would be able to secure the time needed for such a project. "Then, just do 2 pages," I countered back. One month later, I had the first draft of the book you hold in your hands. Knowing Caleb Courtney, I was surprised but not shocked in what he submitted to me.

Caleb was the right person to write this book. He and his wife, Stephanie, and family, have faithfully attended Bethel now for over 11 years. Together, they have provided anointed leadership to our worship ministry all these years. Caleb has served, many of those years, with excellence as an Elder in our church. They are a couple that is greatly respected by both young and old at Bethel. But even more than that, Caleb is a diligent student, with a deep interest in history, particularly Canadian Pentecostal history. This interest is more than just information of dates and stories, but coupled with it is a sincere passion for a renewed Pentecostal experience today.

Caleb has provided a great blessing to Bethel in the writing of this book. I am afraid much of it might have been lost without his diligence to provide this written history. I am reminded of the Scripture in Psalms 78:4-6 which reads: "Tell the generation to come the praises of the Lord, and His strength and His wonderful works that He has done. For He established a testimony in Jacob *(note: God has established a testimony in Sarnia)* ... that the generation to come might know them ... that they may set their hope in God, and not forget the works of God."

As I read through this historical account of the History of Bethel Pentecostal Church in Sarnia, Ontario, I clearly see the faithfulness of God along with the faithfulness of His people. What blesses me the most is that after all these years, Bethel has not lost its original DNA. Bethel Pentecostal Church in Sarnia began with a passion for local outreach and missions work with an emphasis on the presence and power of the Holy Spirit. Bethel today continues in that same passion. The Vision has not been lost and I believe that the best days for Bethel are yet to come!

Pastor Tim Gibb
Lead Pastor, Bethel Pentecostal Church
2004 to Present

Acknowledgments

This past summer, I was doing some research at the Pentecostal Assemblies of Canada Archives in Mississauga, Ontario, and had refreshed my memory of Bethel's history. Shortly thereafter, I attended Braeside Camp, and posted a brief memory to Facebook:

Caleb Courtney at 📍 Braeside Pentecostal Camp.
July 11

In 1938, Sarnia Pastor, Mrs. Edna Riblet went to Braeside Camp in Paris, Ontario and was filled with the Holy Spirit. In March 1941, the "Sarnia Gospel Mission" (which she began in 1936 as a Free Methodist) affiliated with the Pentecostal Assemblies of Canada. The "Sarnia Gospel Mission" is now known as Bethel Pentecostal Church in Sarnia, Ontario. (Photo is from an old post card).

👍 Like   💬 Comment   ↗ Share

Almost immediately, I received a message from Pastor Tim Gibb saying, "Did we miss the reality that it is Bethel's 80ᵗʰ anniversary this year?" This was followed by a request asking if I would please consider doing four video segments and a brief article on Bethel's eighty-year history. I was just finishing a Master's degree in Theological Studies, and had about a hundred pages of final assignments left to write. I wrote back that I would love to do it, but didn't know when I would have the time to do it with all of my other responsibilities. Pastor Tim ignored the latter part of my reply and wrote back facetiously, "So you're saying yes! Awesome!"

In truth, I had wanted to write a history of Bethel Pentecostal Church in Sarnia for some time. I love that women have played such an instrumental role in our history. I love that there are consistent themes, such as strong faith, an expectancy for miracles, an emphasis on missions, and a loving concern for the local community. In writing this history, I have taken many hours to research at the Sarnia Library, looking through city directories and old newspapers on microfilm. I have been in contact with local historians in Sarnia, and while none had heard of a "Shanty Town" in Sarnia in the 1930's, they were very interested that it had been mentioned in a national publication, *The Pentecostal Testimony*, during that decade.

Jim Craig, the archivist at the PAOC Archives has been a significant help to me, graciously fielding my many requests. Ben Wright of Master's Pentecostal Seminary has openly shared his knowledge and resources with me. Dr. Van Johnson has been a friend and mentor throughout my pursuit of a graduate degree in Pentecostal Studies, and has called me "Detective Caleb" more than once. Dr. Marty Mittelstadt, also a friend, sent me a copy of the article about Barbara Johnston, whom you will meet in a few pages. These people all have my gratitude for their help and encouragement. Pastor Tim, and the members of Bethel who have shared their stories, also have my thanks. I have been present for only the last eleven of the eighty years of Bethel's history, so I have had to rely on past written records and the current memories of those who were there in the early days.

My wife, Stephanie, regularly reminds me of the importance of adequate sleep, proofreads my written work, and is ever an encourager to me. She will always have my heart. My kids, Olivia, Sam, Marcus, and Joel, who joke about my fondness for the many "Pentecostal books" that fill my bookshelves, fill my life with joy. I thank my parents and in-laws for raising us to be Pentecostal people in theology and experience. We hope to give our children the same gift. Of course, my Lord and Saviour, Jesus Christ, who has baptized me in the Holy Ghost, and is coming soon, ever deserves my grateful praise and enthusiastic worship. May Bethel's history testify of God's faithfulness to all generations, and to him be all the glory.

Caleb Courtney
Sarnia, Ontario, Canada
December 2016

Part of a 1937-38 Roadmap of the Province Ontario.
Sarnia is located at the southernmost tip of Lake Huron.

1

Introduction

KNOWN HISTORY

For several decades, Bethel Pentecostal Church in Sarnia, Ontario, has quite correctly traced its roots to a small Sunday School started by Edna Riblet on White Street in the summer of 1936. Following that, the church moved to 245 Essex Street, and then on to 1565 London Line. However, this is only a partial history of Pentecostalism in Sarnia. The Pentecostal message had found a place in Sarnia several decades earlier, as early as August 1908.

WHAT IS "PENTECOSTAL"?

What does it mean to be Pentecostal? It is certainly much more than simply being a Christian who speaks in tongues. Pentecostals have a very high view of the authority of the Bible. They have a high Christology, understanding that Jesus is God incarnate, and that he is their Saviour, Spirit Baptizer, Healer, and Soon Coming King. Out of this understanding, Pentecostals respond with gratitude and often unbridled enthusiasm in worship. Worship extends beyond their meetings and into the way they live their lives, with an emphasis on personal holiness. Pentecostals believe that the signs and wonders performed by Jesus and the apostles are equally—and even more so—available for believers today. The expression of spontaneous spiritual gifts in a church service, while to an outsider might seem chaotic, are for the Pentecostal believer an indicator of divine order, and that the Holy Spirit is in control.

Pentecostals celebrate when the Holy Spirit speaks through the laity in tongues and interpretation, prophecy, and exhortations. Discernment is used by the community when hearing such messages, as the words are always judged by the authority of Scripture. At the turn of the twentieth century, the early Pentecostals believed that that they were living in "the last of the last days," and that the second coming of the Lord was imminent. It was thus an urgent necessity to devote one's life to missionary service, whether at home or abroad. These Pentecostal churches were end-time focussed, spiritually vibrant, enthusiastic, spontaneous, worshipping, missional, and above all, Scriptural, communities.

AZUSA STREET, LOS ANGELES

Many Pentecostal churches trace their roots to the Azusa Street Revival, an amazing Spirit-filled revival that began in Los Angeles on April 18, 1906.[1] It was a dramatic and spectacular event of global significance. While Pentecostals make no special observance of this date, it is a part of our shared identity and history. The *Los Angeles Herald* reported that the participants in the Azusa Street Revival were "all ages, sexes, colors, nationalities and previous conditions of servitude"[2]—a poignant statement in an era that emphasized segregation by skin color and inequality based on numerous social factors. This revival, though several thousand kilometres away, touched Canada. In 1907 and 1908, the Azusa Street Revival's newsletter, *The Apostolic Faith*, published Pentecostal testimonies that had been written by people in Toronto, Ontario,[3] Snowflake, Manitoba,[4] and Melfort, Saskatchewan.[5]

CANADIAN PENTECOSTAL ORIGINS

In Canada, three geographic centers of Pentecostal revival emerged, along with its leaders: R. E. McAlister in Ottawa, Ellen Hebden in Toronto, and A. H. Argue and his family in Winnipeg. Ellen Hebden is the first person known to have received Pentecostal baptism in Canada.[6]

In her newsletter, *The Promise*, she writes about how Pentecost came to Toronto, and how on November 17, 1906, she was baptized in the Holy Spirit and spoke in other tongues. Mrs. Hebden's testimony has been included at the end of this book in its entirety, and is typical of many Pentecostal testimonies of the time.[7] Her husband James writes in the same newsletter, "Since November 17th God has been wonderfully blessing and baptizing His children with the Holy Spirit, and giving the gift of Tongues."[8] He encourages their readers to seek God above all else. "There is a tendency with the people to be seeking to speak with Tongues rather than to seek the Baptism, and the Baptism rather than the Baptizer. Above all things seek Him. He shall baptize you with the Holy Ghost and Fire, and ye shall be witnesses."[9] Both the Hebdens and the Argues played an important part of Pentecostalism in Sarnia, although their influence here has been all but forgotten.

Pentecostal newsletters: The Promise *was issued by James and Ellen Hebden of Toronto from 1907-1910;* The Revival Broadcast *was issued by A. H. Argue and his family of Winnipeg from 1923-1928.*

2

Sarnia's First Pentecostal Missionary

Barbara Norton, née Johnston,[10] was the daughter of John Johnston, a prominent principal and teacher in the city of Sarnia who, upon his death, had a school named after him—Johnston Memorial Public School (which was torn down several years ago, and is now the site of P. E. McGibbon Public School).[11] In a recently rediscovered newsletter article from 1909 in India, Barbara describes her childhood calling into overseas missions:

> I was brought up in a Christian home in Sarnia, Ontario, Canada. My mother gave me to the Lord at my birth. When I was about eight years old, two young out-going missionaries addressed our Sunday-School, and as they spoke of the needs of India my heart burned within me, and I said to myself, "Someday I hope I can go to India, to tell the people about Jesus." I was not converted till two years later, but that desire never left me.[12]

Several years later, having just graduated from McMaster University in Toronto,[13] Miss Johnston did not immediately move back to Sarnia as expected. She was believing to be baptized with the Holy Ghost and speak in other tongues. She graduated on May 15, 1907, but in her own words, her newly earned degree "seemed of little value compared with the blessing I was seeking." Barbara writes that she stayed in Toronto, and prayed earnestly for this blessing in the "upper room" of the Hebdens' East End Mission at 651 Queen Street East, only five kilometres from the university:

> After my graduation I still tarried on, learning lessons of faith and patience, and on May 29th, while praying, the Lord directed my

attention to the two promises—"If ye then being evil know how to give good gifts to your children, how much more shall your heavenly father give the Holy Spirit to them that ask him." Luke 11:13, and also, "And this is the confidence which we have in him, that, if we ask anything according to his will, he heareth us; and if we know that he hears us whatsoever we ask, we know that we have the petitions that we desired of him." I John 5:14, 15. Quick as a flash, I saw "It must be according to his will because he has promised." I asked believing that I received, and the Lord's power was wonderfully manifested. After about two months waiting, I seemed to have reached the point where I could reach out and receive by faith. For the next two days I waited in quite expectancy for the Lord to manifest his presence according to his word. In the upper room, 651 Queen St. East, Toronto, on Friday afternoon, May 31st, the Lord came to me again in great power, and in the evening spoke through me in another tongue. Then I knew the work was finished. The Lord said to me "Go home to thy friends and tell them what great things the Lord has done for thee." I went home and tried to obey.[14]

The home Miss Johnston mentions was 286 College Street in Sarnia, Ontario, where she boarded with her father.[15] She taught for one year at a school in the country, and gathered with a "small company" of people for regular Pentecostal meetings. We know little about these meetings or where they were held, and whether this "small company" existed before Miss Johnston arrived or if she initiated this group upon her arrival. In any case, having had theological training at McMaster University, and having experienced the baptism of the Holy Spirit, she ended up leading the group. The following year, in August 1908, James and Ellen Hebden came from Toronto to Sarnia, and were instrumental in confirming the Lord's will for Miss Johnston's life:

> In August 1908 Mr. and Mrs. Hebden, from the Queen East Mission, where I had received the baptism, came to Sarnia to hold some meetings. It was just a few days before my school should start, and I was engaged there till the end of the year. One day I went around to the house where the Hebdens were staying, and found Mrs. Hebden lying on the couch, with closed eyes, talking in tongues such beautiful poetry.

When I went in she was interpreting. She said "They are calling— They
are calling to thee— They are calling from over the sea. The time of
separation is coming for thee." Then came the word "India" and I knew
it was for me. She went on "The Lord will open the way. Man closes up,
but the Lord will open the way." I knew how true that was. Then she
said again "The time of separation is coming for thee."[16]

This cemented the missionary call to India for Miss Johnston,
but she could not leave her school without a teacher, or the Pentecostal
mission without a leader. Within the first two weeks of the school term, a
new teacher arrived at the school, and a man came to assume leadership
of the mission, both of which were a response to her prayers. On
November 7, 1908, Miss Johnston left for India, where she assisted
world-renowned missionary Pandita Ramabai and her Mukti Mission.
Ramabai worked closely with Albert and Mary Norton, who operated a
mission in Dhond, India. In January 1909, the Norton's missionary
newsletter announced:

Miss Barbara Johnstone from Sarnia, Canada ... has gone on to
Kedgaon and is working as a helper to Pandita Ramabai in the Mukti
Mission. She has received the Baptism of the Holy Spirit, and speaks in
tongues fluently.[17]

Barbara Johnston soon married the Nortons' son, John. In
January of 1912, the Mukti Mission published news of her death, only
three years after her arrival in India.

Mrs. John Norton is now among the names of those who are with the
King. Some of our readers will remember that Miss Barbara Johnstone
of Sarnia, Ontario, worked with us here for a little while, and was
afterwards married to Mr. John Norton of Dhond.

Mrs. John Norton helped us in many ways, chiefly in the Greek work
connected with the Bible Translation. She was a graduate of Toronto
University. At the Master's call she left all, and followed him to India, to
live a Christ-like life among simple village men and women, devoting
all her time and talents to the work of revealing Christ to them, that
they might "Look and Live."[18]

Barbara A. Johnston, wife of John E. Norton, lived from 1879 to 1911, and was Sarnia's first known Pentecostal missionary. She died in India at the age of 32, less than two years into her marriage, and was buried in the Johnston family plot at Lakeview Cemetery in Sarnia. Her personal testimony is included in its entirety at the end of this book, as originally published in 1909.

372　　　*The McMaster University Monthly.*

BARBARA JOHNSTONE.

"Enflamed with the study of learning."

Barbara Johnstone just missed being born a Yankee by half a mile, Sarnia being her birthplace. While she was yet a child a trip across the St. Clair River into Uncle Sam's domain was one of her Saturday afternoon delights. On these little journeys her never-failing companion was a separate leaf note-book, in which she jotted down voluminous data on everything imaginable. This habit of taking notes became chronic and afflicted her during her early education in Sarnia, and has caused many a "brain-storm" among the professors at McMaster, who have occasionally come into collision with the facts as set down in her black book.

Intends to be—A teacher. Spends her idle moments—Writing essays. Pet phrase—? ? ? ? ? ?

Barbara Johnston's 1907 graduation photo in the graduation edition of The McMaster University Monthly.[19] *She experienced the baptism in the Holy Spirit on May 31, 1907—sixteen days after graduating from McMaster University—and heard the Lord say to her "Go home to thy friends [in Sarnia] and tell them what great things the Lord has done for thee."*

3

The Earliest Pentecostal Churches in Sarnia

Johnston's mention of a small Pentecostal group beginning with her arrival back in Sarnia in 1907 is the first record of any such meeting in Sarnia. From Barbara Johnston's testimony, we know that there was an openness to manifestations of the Spirit among Methodist people in Sarnia as early as 1901. She recalls at that time, "in a Free Methodist meeting, I heard the leader say of people, who I thought were acting strangely, that they were full of the Holy Ghost as on the day of Pentecost." Miss Johnston remembers thinking of the people in Sarnia, "if they would speak with other tongues as they did on the day of Pentecost I would believe they were filled with the Holy Ghost."[20] It is most likely that these Free Methodist people were not speaking in tongues, but were acting strangely Pentecostal in some other way. Certain behaviours—people shaking or jerking while praying, sudden outbursts or shouts of praise, and even people being "slain in the Spirit" or prostrating themselves in prayer—were not uncommon in Free Methodist meetings across North America at the turn of the twentieth century.

For instance, in Topeka, Kansas on January 1, 1901, a young Bible college student named Agnes Ozman spoke in other tongues while in prayer. She was studying the book of Acts while attending the Bible College of Charles Parham, a former Methodist minister who is often considered a "father of the Pentecostal Movement."[21] News of Ozman's experience spread very quickly among Christians who were hungry for a fresh move of the Holy Spirit. Ozman served as a modern-day example of what many had observed in the book of Acts, and what would become a distinctive belief in Pentecostal churches: that the baptism in the Holy Spirit is normally accompanied with the phenomenon of speaking in tongues. This has commonly been called the "initial evidence" of the baptism in the Spirit. Ozman described her experience of speaking in tongues as "the biblical sign" of Spirit baptism,[22] while her teacher, Parham, hailed it as "the indisputable proof" of Spirit baptism.[23] While there has been debate over this doctrine from time to time, all of the major Pentecostal denominations have repeatedly espoused this doctrine on the basis of Scripture and their experience.[24] Thus, at the very same time that Barbara Johnston was considering speaking in tongues as proof of being "full of the Holy Ghost" in Sarnia, Ontario, these ideas were being experienced and documented in Topeka, Kansas.

The first official record of a permanently established Pentecostal church in Sarnia is in 1928. The 1928 *Sarnia City Directory* lists a "Pentecostal Mission" at 165½ Victoria Street North.[25] The "half" of an address at this time usually indicated the upper room of the building, but could also indicate the second side of a duplex. This address was also the location of a "Christian Reading Room."[26] Victoria Street North no longer extends this far, and today this address would likely be located near the fountain in the middle of Sarnia's Bayside Mall between its Lochiel Street entrances. It is unknown who founded or led this first Pentecostal Mission.

It should be noted that Pentecostals used the term "mission" to describe their churches in the early twentieth century.[27] This came from their understanding that the church was primarily defined by its mission to spread the gospel, and not simply for mutual encouragement among Christians. The Pentecostal church was a "missionary fellowship"[28]— every member a missionary. While some Pentecostals might be specifically called to foreign mission fields, Pentecostals believed that every believer was called to local missionary work in their daily life.

In May 1929, there is a brief mention of Sarnia in *The Pentecostal Testimony*, the official magazine of the Pentecostal Assemblies of Canada (PAOC). It reads, quite simply, "A new assembly is being opened Sunday at Sarnia in affiliation with the Pentecostal Assemblies of Canada."[29] A month later, *Testimony* readers are given an update, with more details: "A new Assembly has been opened up at Sarnia. Brother Frank Jolley, a graduate from the Bible School, is pastor in charge. They have a splendid hall, centrally located and the outlook is good for a prosperous Assembly there."[30] Frank Reginald Jolley, born in April 1904, had been raised in the Anglican and Salvation Army traditions.[31] By the time he was seventeen, his parents and siblings had clearly become Pentecostal, declaring so on Canada's 1921 Census.[32] Jolley moved to Sarnia to assume the pastorate as a fresh graduate of the Canadian Pentecostal Bible College in Winnipeg, Manitoba. The location of the "splendid hall, centrally located" was above the Sarnia Hydro Shop at 220½ North Front Street, on the southwest corner of Front and George Streets.

On June 18, 1929, only a month after arriving in Sarnia, Jolley married Alice Moore at the Pentecostal Tabernacle in London, Ontario, with PAOC founder R. E. McAlister officiating.[33] One of the benefits of being in the PAOC fellowship at the time was that it brought a network of connections to other pastors and evangelists. During Jolley's time in Sarnia, several evangelists visited the city, including Miss Edith Gaetz of Hanna, Alberta.[34] The Pentecostal church in Sarnia even produced its own evangelists, as *The Pentecostal Testimony* writes about "Evangelist Harry C. Harris of Sarnia."[35] Jolley, being brand new to pastoral ministry, benefited from fellowship with Pastor Walter McAlister and Gordon Atter[36] who were pastors at the new Pentecostal church just down the rail line in Strathroy at this time.[37] By 1930, Jolley had moved to St. Catharines, Ontario, and while Pentecostal believers in Sarnia likely continued to meet together privately in homes, it seems they did so without a permanent meeting place or pastor for several years.

In the fall of 1934, Sister Adeline Elizabeth Stephan, an evangelist with the PAOC, was given charge of the Pentecostal church in Sarnia.[38] Stephan had established numerous Pentecostal groups around Ontario, including one in Warwick in June 1933. As an evangelist, she had travelled from her home in Strathroy to many of the Pentecostal churches across Canada, and was known for her healing ministry. The history of the Parry Sound Pentecostal Tabernacle records that at one time, "Sis. Adeline Stephan came to fill in until a new pastor came. She was wonderfully used of God in praying for the sick. Many were healed and the spirit of God worked wonderfully through her."[39] One personal account, dating back to some revival services held by Sister Stephan in Bristol Ridge, Quebec, almost a decade earlier in 1924, testifies to the power of God in such meetings:

> For fourteen years I have suffered beyond description, stuttering and stammering so much, I could seldom make myself understood. I attended some Revival Meetings at the Pentecostal Church, Bristol Ridge, conducted by Sister Adeline Stephan, and hearing that Jesus Christ still healed all manner of sickness, I gave my heart to God and was anointed and prayed for, and Glory to God, Jesus has made me every whit whole. He has also baptized me with the Holy Ghost since. Praise His Holy Name. Truly we have a wonderful Saviour. May the Lord bless this testimony to some other souls in need of this wonder-working Jesus. Signed, James F. Kelly, Bristol Ridge, Quebec.[40]

Testimonies like this one give a good idea of what Sister Stephan's meetings were like. These were "Full Gospel" meetings, which highlighted Jesus as the Saviour, Spirit Baptizer, Healer, and Soon Coming King, and people responded to her messages with faith.

In February of 1935, *The Pentecostal Testimony* announced news of Sister Stephans's work in Sarnia with the headline, "Showers of Blessing in Sarnia, Ont." The article continued, "A new work was opened in Sarnia last fall. The Lord giving us an ideal location in the heart of the city."[41] This new location was at 227 North Front Street, only a few doors down and across the street from their previous location, this time above the Union Gas Company of Canada.[42] Today this address is the parking lot for the Bank of Montreal that backs onto Front Street. Perhaps it is fitting that the first Pentecostal churches in Sarnia, who embraced the supernatural power of the Holy Spirit, were located above two sources of natural power—the local hydro and natural gas companies!

Evangelist and pastor Adeline E. Stephan was known for her Holy Spirit filled healing ministry. She pastored a Pentecostal Assemblies of Canada church in the heart of Sarnia from 1934-1948.

The opening service of the new location on November 22, 1934, had several guests. PAOC General Superintendent Rev. James Swanson preached at the service, who was pastoring in Windsor during his administrative appointment within the denomination. From Strathroy, Ontario, Gordon Atter and his wife were in attendance, along with some of their church orchestra and choir. After a few months at this location, the church moved to 163½ South Mitton Street, near the southwest corner of Mitton and Wellington streets. At this location, they were known as the Full Gospel Mission,[43] and there were three Sunday services—Sunday school at 10 AM, followed by the morning service at 11 AM, and then an evening evangelistic service at 7 PM. Visiting evangelists continued to make Sarnia a destination at Sister Stephan's request. *The Pentecostal Testimony* included an update from Sister Stephan in June 1935, where nationally-known evangelists Rev. and Mrs.

Samuel H. Wilson, who had just established a Pentecostal work in Bothwell, Ontario,[44] and Lena Swanson, from Windsor, Ontario, were named:

> Ever since we opened last fall there has been a steady increase both in interest and in numbers. Recently Evangelists S. H. and Mrs. Wilson, conducted revival meetings with us which were so blest of God we felt it advisable to continue with another campaign. At present Sis. Lena Swanson is our evangelist.[45]

Sister Stephan lived and ministered in Sarnia for over twenty years. Early in her ministry in Sarnia, it became Stephan's tradition to hold special nightly evangelistic meetings over the Christmas and New Year's holidays, often turning to the "Argue Evangelistic Party,"[46] the ministry of A. H. Argue's family from Winnipeg, Manitoba. A. H. Argue's daughter, evangelist Zelma Argue, preached at these services in 1934. *The Sarnia Canadian Observer* sometimes summarized these meetings in a small paragraph or two. On Wednesday, January 2, 1934, *The Sarnia Canadian Observer* reported:

> "How Stars Are Made" is the topic tonight of Zelma Argue, Winnipeg evangelist, at the Full Gospel tabernacle, corner of Mitton and Wellington streets. On Monday night pledges were received towards a fund to purchase additional chairs to enlarge the seating capacity, which has been inadequate. This is the final week of the holiday series of services. On Monday night, Miss Argue's farewell address to 1934 was, "Why I Am a Preacher."[47]

Pentecostal evangelist Zelma Argue visited Sarnia frequently in the 1930's.

In 1938, a visiting Pentecostal evangelist made news headlines again, this time achieving the large headline on the local news page of *The Sarnia Canadian Observer.* "Evangelist Helps Save Sarnia Man from Drowning." The visiting evangelist, Elwin Argue, one of A. H. Argue's sons, rescued a man in Sarnia who, while fishing, had fallen through the ice of Sarnia Bay. Attracted by the man's cries for help, Argue, a former lifeguard, rescued the man despite the dangerous condition of the ice. Although the fire department had been called, Argue had already saved the man from drowning. The article begins, "Evangelist Elwin Argue, of Winnipeg, who is conducting a soul-saving campaign in the Full Gospel Tabernacle here ... rescued Joseph St. John ...who fell through the ice of Sarnia Bay while fishing about 200 feet from shore."[48] *The Pentecostal Testimony* also reported the incident to its readers.[49]

The Only Daily Newspaper Published In Lambton

The Sarnia Canadian

SARNIA, ONTARIO, MONDAY, MARCH 14, 1938.

SHIPS' ENGINEERS ARRIVE

Angler Fell Through Ice In Sarnia Bay

EVANGELIST ARGUE TO RESCUE

He And Companion Ventured Across Ice And Shivering Man Was Drawn To The Shore

Evangelist Elwin Argue, of Winnipeg, who is conducting a soul-saving campaign in the Full Gospel Tabernacle here, was one of two men who, yesterday afternoon, rescued Joseph St. John, St. Vincent street, who fell through the ice of Sarnia Bay while fishing about 200 feet from shore. The other rescuer was V. Scully, of Montreal, who is visiting in the city. This was the first rescue from the St. Clair River this year.

By coincidence Mr. Argue is a former lifeguard, who was stationed on Lake Winnipeg, and today he warned the public, particularly children that the ice in the bay is not safe.

BREVITIES FROM HERE AND THERE

SAP RUN GOOD
Farmers in the Jarvis district report the sap has been running well the past few days. Cold nights and bright, sunshiny days contribute to a good yield. One farmer with 500 trees tapped, reports the quality of the syrup is exceptionally good.

SPRING AT GODERICH
Spring arrived at Goderich during the weekend 10 days ahead of schedule. Robins were seen and heard by churchgoers in half a dozen different places. Wild geese winged their way north along Lake Huron shore line, and crows cawed overhead. Robins bits of ice remain in shaded spots and highways are dry.

INJURED IN FALL
Falling over a bank, a distance of probably 30 feet, at the rear of stores on the east side of Thomas street, Ingersoll, Percy Chute, 16, received severe head injuries and had a narrow escape from going into a creek. He received a cut on the right side of the head above the ear and another at the back of the head. He was taken to Alexandra Hospital but his condition is not regarded as serious.

NO VACANT HOUSES
Wheatley, a little town where most of the residents own their homes, has a serious shortage of houses for rent. Not one house is available and vacant space over stores has been turned into apartments recently. Rents have been low and taxes high owing to the

Left Tackle Behind
Mr. St. John, an employe of the Dominion Salt Company, apparently suffered no ill-effects, for he reported for work as usual last night. Shivering with cold the fisherman hurried home as soon as he was removed from the bay and left without taking his fishing equipment.

Mr. Argue was walking near the government warehouse at the harbor, where he heard calls for help. Looking in the direction from which they came he saw a man with only his arms and head above the ice.

"I ran quite a distance before I could get to him and when I got to the evangelist said. "We started out on the ice but when we couldn't reach him we had to get branches of trees which he grabbed, and we eventually were able to pull him out."

Mr. St. John's small son, who was with him, tried to help, but he was unsuccessful. As the fisherman was nearly hysterical and he believed he had been in the water some minutes before being rescued. As soon as he was pulled safely to shore the man and the boy headed north along the railway tracks to home.

Employes of the Sarnia Elevator Company heard the shouts and summoned the fire department rescue squad, but in the meantime the man had been taken from the water.

Issues Warning
Having almost gone through the ice while assisting in the rescue, Mr. Argue warned children against playing on the bay because the ice is too thin. In fact, he said, the ice is not thick enough in some spots, to hold even a child.

In conversation with reporter for The Canadian Observer, Evangelist Argue said he was glad to have been of assistance during his visit to Sarnia.

NEW JAP MINISTER

Baron Tomii, counsellor to the Japanese embassy at London, has been appointed minister to Canada, according to reports issued from there. He will succeed Toshimatsu Kato, who will become minister to Austria.

Adjudicator Of Drama Festival Most Able Man

Barrett H. Clark Ardent Devotee of Both Professional and Amateur Stage

New York, March 14.—Barrett H. Clark, newly appointed adjudicator of the Dominion Drama Festival finals to be held in Winnipeg next May, said yesterday he hopes to see as many Canadian plays as possible in the contest.

Mr. Clark, a native of Toronto, said he has a great interest in and a great admiration for what young Canadian dramatists are doing. There are about 50 authors of one-act dramas in the dominion who are "worth watching," he remarked.

Because of his position as adjudicator, he said he preferred not to mention any names.

Mr. Clark has written several books of theatre criticism, stage history and biography. He also has translated plays from French into English, and once served as an actor and assistant stage man

Liberals Open Drive At Arkona

Riding Is Urged To Return Member Of Government

Arkona, March 14.—(By Staff Reporter)—The Ontario government is considering a proposal to extend the new provincial park at Ipperwash Beach, William Guthrie, M.L.A. Lambton West, told an audience which on Saturday evening assembled to open the Liberal-Progressive party's campaign in the East Lambton by-election. The extension to the park was proposed by Milton D. McVicar, M.L.A. prior to his death.

Records Praised
"The department of lands and forests is giving consideration to the late Mr. McVicar's request," Mr. Guthrie said. "You will recall that it was Mr. McVicar and the Hepburn government which established the One new park at Ipperwash."

Paying tribute to the memory of the late Mr. McVicar Ross W. Gray, K. C., M. P. for Lambton West voiced his surprise that the Conservatives had decided to oppose election of a Liberal-Progressive successor to the late member and that of the present administration were stressed by the speakers. Colin McLeish of Arkona, was chairman of the program.

Paying tribute to the memory of the late Mr. McVicar Ross W. Gray, K. C., M. P. for Lambton West voiced his surprise that the Conservatives had decided to oppose election of a Liberal-Progressive successor to the late member. He said that there had been nothing, which had occurred since October 4 that would necessitate a vote being taken on the issues of provincial politics. He urged the electors of the riding not to send a representative to Queen's Park who would become a member of a minority group.

"The Hon. Earl Rowe, the Conservative leader for Ontario has ordered this riding contested," Mr. Gray concluded. "He takes a hand in this affair and yet he refused the offer of a seat in the provincial legislature where he belongs. We can't get rid of him at Ottawa."

Candidate Speaks
Confidence permeated the address of the candidate, Mr. Fair-

ROYAL AIR FORC[E]

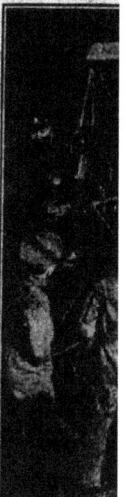

Boys of Denstone Coll aeroplane which has been structional purposes in con an air section with the sch

Sarnia Luml Eight Millio

C. H. Belton Tells Sales Of Extensive Operation ried Out—Dinner Was On Saturday Evening

The Laidlaw, Belton Lumb Ltd., employed 755 men in th in Northern Ontario and to a cut of more than eight feet of timber, C. H. Belton acting director of the company any at a company dinner on day night. The dinner was the sales staff and was giv the Vendome Hotel.

Summarizes Operations
Mr. Belton, who returned fr camps several weeks ago, g brief summary of the oper

---

The Sarnia Canadian Observer on March 14, 1938, featured Pentecostal evangelist Elwin Argue. He was conducting a "soul-saving campaign" and one day rescued a man who had fallen through the ice while fishing in Sarnia Bay.

During the 1930's, Sarnia's newspaper customarily covered the meeting topics featured at all of the city's churches. In Saturday's paper, the residents of Sarnia could view the titles of every sermon that would be preached the next day. Elwin Argue was featured in different ways in these small summaries over his multi-week visit. On February 28, 1938: "Evangelist Elwin Argue, of Winnipeg, noted radio contributor, will conduct these services. Mr. Argue will sing, play, and speak at these services. Strangers and visitors made welcome."[50] In March, he was advertised to be preaching sermons entitled, "Jesus the Son of God," "Two Minutes After Death — What Then?" "Rewards Offered," and "Coming Wars in the Light of Prophecy." He would also be singing "baritone solos," and giving "illustrated talks."[51] According to one eyewitness account, other noted evangelists such as Mark Buntain, Tom Richardson, and "Mr. McAlister" (either R. E. McAlister from London, Ontario, or Walter McAlister from Strathroy, Ontario) also visited Sarnia.[52]

Weekly notices like these appeared in The Sarnia Canadian Observer *throughout the 1920's and 1930's. From left to right: May 25, 1929, June 15, 1929, and February 26, 1938.*

While many evangelists visited Sarnia, a few evangelists were called from the Pentecostal congregation in Sarnia as well. In 1936, evangelist Charles Forrest, from Sarnia, left to assist the Wilsons in their efforts in Bothwell, where their church had grown to include more than one hundred people.[53] Arthur and Letitia Williams, the parents of Rev. Earl Williams and Dr. Randall Williams, are listed among the early

Spirit-filled Pentecostals in Sarnia. Rev. Max Powers,[54] who became a missionary to Africa from Sarnia, was a Pentecostal who had experienced the baptism in the Holy Spirit.[55]

By 1941, the Full Gospel Tabernacle had moved to 241 Lochiel Street, on the southwest corner of Lochiel and Euphemia streets. This is where Sister Stephan ministered until the late forties, when this church would become a part of Bethel Pentecostal Church.

Left: 163 (left half) and 161 (right half) Mitton Street South. The building has a concrete stone at the top that reads "F. Daws Block." 163½ Mitton Street South (likely the top of the left half) was the location of the Full Gospel Tabernacle led by Sister A. E. Stephan from 1934 until sometime in 1939 or 1940.

Right: 241 Lochiel Street is now a parking lot (top right), but in some places, the original foundation can still be seen (bottom right). 241 Lochiel Street was the location of the Full Gospel Tabernacle led by Sister A. E. Stephan from 1941 to 1948, when it merged with Bethel Pentecostal Church.

Parallel to the development of PAOC-affiliated Pentecostal churches in the 1920's and 1930's, another Pentecostal mission was opened at 467 George Street, on the corner of George Street and North Russell Street, led by W. James McKeown.[56] This mission was not affiliated with the PAOC or Sister Stephan's work, but rather the Apostolic Church in Canada,[57] a Pentecostal denomination that has its roots in the Welsh Revival of 1904-1905. With a slightly different emphasis than the PAOC, the Apostolic Church in Sarnia focussed on the fivefold ministry of Apostles, Prophets, Evangelists, Pastors, and Teachers. This church operated until the mid-1980's, at which time several of its members subsequently found a new home church at Bethel, even serving as board members. The building on George Street, which retains much of its original shape and structure today, is now FairHavens Baptist Church.

4

The White Street Mission & Edna Riblet

The White Street Mission is where the story of Bethel Pentecostal Church usually begins, but is really a parallel story to what had already been happening in Sarnia. In 1936, while Sister Stephan continued to faithfully carry on a Pentecostal work in central Sarnia, a Free Methodist widow by the name of Edna Riblet began to teach the Bible to young boys and girls under a hawthorn tree on White Street. White Street, which today is known as Oxford Street, was at this time outside the Sarnia city limits, in Sarnia Township. At the time, the entrance gate to the city of Sarnia was on London Road at East Street. Today the side posts of these gates can be found at the entrance of Canatara Park on Christina Street. In the 1930's, during the Great Depression, White Street was an impoverished area on the outskirts of town where most of the houses were more aptly described as "shanties"—makeshift lodgings that might resemble houses, but generally without many amenities. Most of the residents in this neighbourhood were on relief rolls from the government.

This photo of children under a tree is from Edna Riblet's personal photo collection, and is labelled, "Mission Sunday School."

Entrance to Sarnia, Ontario, Canada.—4.

*A postcard featuring the entrance to the city of Sarnia,
facing west, on London Road at East Street. The White
Street Mission was located two blocks east and one block
north of this location, outside the city, in Sarnia Township.*

Edna Riblet (née Gibson) was born on May 8, 1890 in Sombra
Township to William and Margaret Gibson. Her parents were saved
under the "old-fashioned fire-baptized"[58] preaching of Rev. David Allan
at a Free Methodist camp meeting held in 1899 at "Haley's Grove"[59] in
Terminus, Ontario—a small community about forty kilometers south of
Sarnia on the Kimball Road near Duthill. Edna was the fifth of seven
daughters, and had a younger brother who died of an illness at the age of
20.[60] She married John Riblet on December 31, 1908 in Lucas County,
Ohio.[61] Sadly, her husband died only seven years into their marriage.

Edna ended up working from home as a dressmaker,[62] living with—and caring for—her parents in Sarnia, both of whom passed away by 1930.

In 1936, in her mid-forties, Edna felt a strong call to minister to the poor by bringing them the gospel. She set out to start a Sunday School in this poor neighbourhood just outside of the city of Sarnia. The first week she had about a dozen or so children, but the following Sunday afternoon there were forty-three children waiting for her under the hawthorn tree.[63] That winter, a family in the neighbourhood offered the use of their home for these Sunday School meetings. Soon after, a parcel of land with a building was being sold for back taxes on the north end of White Street. Mr. and Mrs. Charles Bell, members of the Free Methodist church in Sarnia, bought this and donated it to Edna's Sunday School mission to the poor. They also supplied everything that was needed to continue meeting indoors: an organ, stove, seats, and some teaching supplies.

Although Edna was a Free Methodist, she was no stranger to the Pentecostal movement which had existed in Sarnia for at least three decades. The Free Methodist church, in fact, was generally quite open to the renewed focus that the Pentecostals had brought to the work of the Holy Spirit. At the time, Free Methodists also enjoyed Bible-based camp-meeting style preaching, like that of the Pentecostals. Two of Edna Riblet's friends were Mrs. Etta Kemsley, who often led the music at the Pentecostal church in Sarnia, and would later become the volunteer song leader at the White Street Mission, and Jessie Leghorn, of the Salvation Army in Sarnia. These friends convinced Edna to attend the new Braeside Pentecostal Camp in Paris, Ontario.

Vol. 16   (60c per year)   TORONTO, JUNE, 1935   (Published Monthly)   Number 6

This masthead from The Pentecostal Testimony *in 1935 demonstrates a focus on the Four-Fold, or "Full" Gospel message of Jesus with Salvation, the Holy Spirit, Healing, and the Second Coming.*

The Western Ontario District of the PAOC had established Braeside in 1935, and "it was the first camp ground to be owned by Pentecostal people in the Dominion of Canada."[64] News had spread quickly about people being saved, people being filled with the Holy Ghost and speaking with tongues, and many believers praying around the altars "long and late."[65] In the summer of 1938, Edna went to Braeside Camp,[66] and was baptized in the Holy Spirit and spoke in other tongues. She returned to Sarnia, preaching the Full Gospel message—Jesus as Saviour, Spirit-Baptizer, Healer, and Soon Coming King.[67] Scholars of Pentecostalism have identified that this fourfold pattern expresses most clearly and cleanly the distinct emphases of Pentecostal theology.[68]

Braeside Camp, near Paris, Ontario, in July 1937. The big
building is the old tabernacle, with large letters above the
doors announcing "Braeside Camp."

Edna Riblet and
a friend at
Braeside Camp
in the summer
of 1938.

Typical scenes at Braeside Camp in the 1930's.
Above: outside the tabernacle. Below: inside the tabernacle.

The Sunday School continued to grow, not only with more children, but with adults as well. Edna often held special services throughout the week, and would regularly visit with people in the neighbourhood, always praying with them before she left their homes. Some referred to her as "strange" because she would often break into tears while praying for others, as she desired so greatly for them to know Jesus as she did.[69]

A photo of the Sunday School in 1938. Among those in the photo are Almer McCabe (tallest in back row), Frank Burden Jr. (2nd last in back row), Frank Burden, Sr. (last in back row); Bruce McCabe (4th in middle row), Stuart Macklin (2nd last in middle row); Carl McCabe (2nd in front row), Martin McCabe (3rd in front row).

In 1938, the same year that the first span of the Blue Water Bridge was completed, Edna purchased a new lot for the church with her own savings, just down the street from the previous property. On the condition that she was using the lot expressly as a church, the township donated three other lots and installed the electricity for the building at no cost. The old church was moved to the corner of what is now Lincoln Park and Oxford Street, and its capacity was expanded to seat up to 150 people at one time. At its completion it was commonly known as the "White Street Mission," although the sign out front simply said "S. S. Mission" (Sunday School Mission).[70] On June 2, 1939, Edna received credentials as a Deaconess with the PAOC. Edna became intentional about collaborating with Sister Stephan for various evangelistic efforts in Sarnia. Sister Stephan, having been invited to preach at the White Street Mission in 1939, is said to have looked out at the hundred or so young faces that had gathered there and wept.[71]

The White Street Mission, which was located on the corner of what is now Oxford Street and Lincoln Park in Sarnia. The black sign on the right appears to list the service times, and declares that "all are welcome."

Somewhere along the way, Edna met James Lewis Hammond from Dunnville, Ontario.[72] A recent widower, Edna fell in love with him, and they soon made plans to get married. In addition to this, Edna had suffered a mild heart attack and needed to find someone to pastor the mission. The White Street Mission could not afford a pastor. Edna had lived on very little, and had given all of her own finances to the work of the church already. Early in 1941, wanting the White Street Mission to continue, Edna and her treasurer, Frank Burden, applied for the church to become affiliated with the PAOC. On March 18, 1941, J. H. Blair, the district superintendent of the Western Ontario District of the PAOC, approved their application. In December of that year, *The Pentecostal Testimony* published an update from Edna, summarizing the renovations of the church, and indicated, despite a lack of financial resources, their zeal to support PAOC missions as a new part of the fellowship:

> We have built two Sunday School rooms at the back, painted the building inside and out and put on a new roof. Much of the work has been donated, and we are nearly clear of debt. God has been blessing in the service here. We are anxious to co-operate with all, with special interest in the Missionary program.[73]

Edna Riblet, the foundress of the White Street Sunday School Mission.

In line with Edna's wishes to hand over the mission to new leadership, the district appointed Rev. Almond Obadiah Routley[74] to become the pastor of the White Street Mission in 1941. He had been living in Toronto and traveling as an itinerant evangelist, and relocated together with his wife, Lydia, and their children to Sarnia, Ontario as his first pastorate. A former car salesman, and an "old-time Methodist,"[75] A. O. Routley had been saved, baptised in the Holy Spirit, and prompted to go into Pentecostal evangelistic ministry, applying for credentials with the PAOC at the age of 42. Like Edna, he agreed that until the church was out of debt, he would support his family with any money left in the church's account after the monthly bills had been paid.

The Polymer Corporation came to Sarnia in 1942, and the city boomed with its success. The company produced artificial rubber in the absence of overseas supplies which were cut off because of World War II.[76] The church soon emerged from its debt. Under A. O. Routley's leadership, from 1941 to 1946, the White Street Mission accumulated a building fund of three thousand dollars,[77] a significant sum of money at the time. In 1946, the Routley family moved fifty kilometres south to pastor in Wallaceburg, Ontario.[78]

A. O. Routley, pictured here in the late 1930's.

[Scanned 11/2014]   5450   SARNIA GOSPEL MISSION ?

APPLICATION of ASSEMBLIES CLOSED

FOR AFFILIATION WITH
THE PENTECOSTAL ASSEMBLIES OF CANADA

Am't Enc'l.............
Receipt No.............
MAR 6 1941
Ans'd. Mar. 18/41

1. Location of Church __White Street__
   (If in Rural District, give nearest P.O.)

2. Street Address of Church (or Rural Route) __Sarnia Township__

3. Name of Church __Gospel Mission__

4. Number of Enrolled Members __Fiveteen__

5. Average Attendance { Sunday A.M. __25__
                        { Sunday P.M. __40__

6. Has the Assembly been organized and church officers appointed? __yes__

7. Name of Secretary of Assembly __Mr Frank Burden__

8. Full Address of Secretary __Sarnia R Route__

9. Name of Pastor of Assembly __Mrs Edna Riblet__

10. Full Address of Pastor __374 N. Russell St__

Sunday School
100 on Roll
80 per cent average

(Signed)   __F.S. Burden__
                 (Secretary)

             __Mrs Edna Riblet__
                 (Pastor)

OFFICIAL ENDORSEMENT

(Have your District Field Officer personally endorse your application for affiliation under this space. If you do not know who your nearest District Officer is, write to Head Office, 362 Danforth Avenue, Toronto, Ontario.)

"I hereby endorse and recommend the Assembly above named for recognition as a P.A.O.C. Assembly, on behalf of the __Western Ontario District__ District of The Pentecostal Assemblies of Canada."

(Signed)   __J.H. Blair__
                 (District Officer)

The Application for Affiliation of the White Street Mission with the PAOC in 1941 by Pastor Edna Riblet and Secretary Frank Burden. Courtesy of the PAOC Archives.

5

Bethel Pentecostal Church at 245 Essex Street

In 1946, Frank R. Jolley and his wife, Alice, returned to pastor in Sarnia. This must have seemed full-circle for them as Sarnia had been their first official pastorate within the PAOC fellowship several years previous in 1929. With the money in the building fund, Jolley led the White Street Mission in purchasing two lots side-by-side on Essex Street. With the prospect of moving to a new location, the congregation decided a new name was in order: Bethel Pentecostal Church. The cornerstone was laid in the fall of 1948, with Rev. Earl Williams of Essex speaking at the event.[79] Since this new church building was now within a kilometre of the Full Gospel Mission run by Adeline Stephan, the two churches joined together. The Thompsons, including a young Joyce Thompson, who would later become Joyce Gingrich, Bethel's pianist for over fifty years, came from Sister Stephan's church.[80] Sister Stephan, now without her own church to pastor, continued as an itinerant evangelist for several years, officially retiring in 1952.[81] She died on February 9, 1957 in her late seventies, and is buried at Lakeview Cemetery in Sarnia.

The first phase of 245 Essex Street was completed in late 1948—a basement only—and could accommodate two hundred people. It was built by Curran and Herridge Contractors of Sarnia. The church held an open house for the public and all city pastors on Friday, December 14, and then celebrated its official opening a few days later, on Sunday, December 16, 1948. This was the first building dedicated with the name "Bethel Pentecostal Church." Rev. W. Fitch, of Windsor, brought a dedicatory message and prayer that Sunday morning, and then spoke again Sunday evening to a "well-filled church."[82] The following Monday, a Western Ontario District PAOC Rally was held in the new building, and was "packed to capacity" for both services. District superintendent J. H. Blair spoke at the services. The ladies of the church served meals to the out-of-town visitors, and an additional $2,000.00 was raised in cash and pledges for the next phase of the church—its main floor auditorium. The pledges were to be paid during the coming year. In an update to *The Pentecostal Testimony* about these events following, Frank Jolley writes, "We are off to a good start, appreciating the convenience and comfort of our new building, and very thankful the Lord for His blessing."[83]

NEW CHURCH DEDICATED AT SARNIA, ONTARIO

The new Bethel Pentecostal Church, located on Essex Street, in Sarnia, Ontario, was opened on December 16th. Rev. W. Fitch, of Windsor, brought the Dedicatory message and prayer on Sunday morning. He also spoke on Sunday evening to a well-filled church. The following Monday the District Rally was held in the new building. Again the place was packed to capacity, and it was a great day! The ladies of the church served meals to all out-of-town visitors. The amount of $2,000.00 was raised in cash and pledges—the pledges to be paid during the coming year. The District Superintendent, Rev. J. H. Blair, brought the message at both services on Monday.

A few months previous Rev. Earl Williams, of Essex, was present and spoke at the laying of the corner-stone of the new church. On December 14th, the Friday evening previous to the official opening, we held an "Open House" for all city pastors and visitors.

We are off to a good start, appreciating the convenience and comfort of our new building, and very thankful to the Lord for His blessing.

—Pastor F. R. Jolley

New church building dedicated at Sarnia, Ont.

March 15, 1949   Page Fifteen

This article appeared in The Pentecostal Testimony *on March 15, 1949. The church looked this way until 1954.*

An artist's sketch of Frank R. Jolley.

In the same vein as the previous Pentecostal churches, Bethel regularly held special nightly evangelistic services. In 1949, Bethel held nightly services for two weeks in April with Rev. C. Nelson from Kitchener, and for three weeks in June with internationally-known Canadian evangelist C. S. Tubby, who operated powerfully in the gift of prophecy.[84] In more recent decades, the Pentecostal church has enjoyed acceptance among the many other Christian denominations, but this has not always been the case. In the first half of the twentieth century, Pentecostals were sometimes seen as "crazy" by the public and by other Christians. In some cities across North America, people complained about the loud music, the constant noise of prayer, spontaneous shrieks and shouts, and services going into all hours of the night—all of which were usually true.[85] Joyful praise and unfettered expressions of worship in the Pentecostal church were seen by some Christians as irreverent or too emotional. Rumours abounded about people swinging from chandeliers and Pentecostal church services were much less liturgical than what people were used to. While there is no specific written record of these opinions specifically in Sarnia, this would have been a part of the general public's preconception of Pentecostals at this time. Thus, it is significant when Pastor Jolley writes that such prejudices were broken down over the course of these special services in 1949: "There was very good attendance, a goodly number of new folk came out night after night and prejudice was broken down."[86]

Edna Riblet, who was now Edna Hammond, moved back to Sarnia around this time. She had ministered with her husband in Dunnville at the "Highway Gospel Mission," but sadly, this second marriage, like her first, lasted only a few years, cut short by her husband's death. James Hammond died in 1948, at the age of sixty-five. Edna, now twice a widow, returned to her roots as a Sunday School teacher in what was now Bethel Pentecostal Church, but without any other ministerial or leadership responsibilities.[87]

Frank Jolley pastored at Bethel longer than any other place he would pastor in his life. He went on to pastor in Sault Ste. Marie for a year, followed by several years of evangelistic and secular work. He died in Kitchener on March 18, 1962, a month shy of his fifty-eighth birthday, having preached twenty-seven times the previous year as a relief pastor, while simultaneously maintaining a secular job.

On May 21, 1953, a devastating F4 tornado hit Sarnia. It damaged over 250 buildings, many of them only a few blocks from the church, but left the church unscathed. This same year, Rev. Robert Norcross, Sr., and his wife Jessie, came to Bethel Pentecostal Church in Sarnia. They had previously pastored in Parry Sound, Elora, and Galt.[88] Mrs. Norcross was the church song leader, and "sometimes got so blessed that she danced a little behind the pulpit turning in a little circle and speaking in tongues and worshipping God."[89] In a history of the Parry Sound Pentecostal Tabernacle, written in 1972, the authors write of the Norcrosses:

> Bro. and Sis. Robert Norcross Sr. moved to Parry Sound around 1934 from Toronto, Ontario and he worked here as meat manager at the Dominion Store. After he was converted he had a battle with the smoking habit and was unable to break this yoke in his own strength but with God all things are possible. One night the Lord gloriously

baptized him in the Holy Spirit and instantly delivered him from the smoking habit, 'Praise God.' The Lord called them into full time ministry ... [and] all of their five children are in full time ministry.[90]

Also in 1953, Charlie Routley, a son of A. O. Routley,[91] became the church's Sunday School Superintendent.

Upon the Norcross's arrival, Pastor Norcross began the process to complete the main floor of the church at 245 Essex Street. The project cost $42,000 and was coordinated by contractor Harry Tosh, a member of the church.[92] It officially opened on April 17, 1954, with an increased seating capacity that could accommodate up to three hundred and fifty people.

The main floor sanctuary of Bethel Pentecostal Church at its 245 Essex Street location.

PENTECOSTAL

BETHEL PENTECOSTAL CHURCH
245 Essex St.

REV. R. NORCROSS, Pastor   Phone ED. 7-2543

SUNDAY SERVICES PASTOR NORCROSS

10.00 A.M.—Sunday School Hour.

11.00 A.M.—

Rev. J. H. Blair
District Superintendent of
Pentecostal Assemblies of Canada.

12.00 NOON—Dedication of new
Parsonage.

7.00 P.M.—

Rev. and Mrs.
J. H. Blair

- - - - - - - - - - - - - - - -

Commencing Next Week
Tuesday, Wednesday and Thursday, 8 p.m.
Great Revival Meetings with

Evangelist
Kenneth Bombay

Friday — 8 p.m.

Gigantic Young People's Rally.
District Churches participating with
Kenneth Bombay speaking.

A large ad in the Sarnia Observer, *November 5, 1960.*[93]

In 1960, Tosh again coordinated the construction of a parsonage next door to the church at 241 Essex Street. This was used by Pastor and Mrs. Norcross immediately upon its completion. Pastor Norcross was a man of prayer and faith. During his pastorate in Sarnia, he was diagnosed with cancer, hospitalized, and given only two months to live. The church board covered the ministerial duties at the church for a short time, but Norcross was miraculously healed of cancer and returned to ministry.

In 1956, Dorothy Dunne, was invited to the Pentecostal church to play the organ. She was a twenty-eight-year-old classically trained pianist who had been singing in choirs and playing the piano at various churches in Sarnia. Dorothy was attracted by the lively music, becoming good friends with the church pianist, Joyce Gingrich. Dorothy was soon baptized in the Holy Spirit and spoke in other tongues. She continued to play the organ at Bethel's services for over sixty years until her death May 23, 2016. The City of Sarnia and Bethel recognized Dorothy's contribution to the church only one month before her death, awarding her with certificates and public appreciation. She was also featured in a front-page article in the local newspaper, *The Sarnia Observer*,[94] which is reprinted in full at the back of this book.

Dorothy Dunne, the church organist from 1956-2016.

Dorothy once told the story of how her two-year-old daughter had been diagnosed with meningitis.

> I won't easily forget when my 2-year-old Martha came down with meningitis. We were at the hospital on Sunday night when they gave us the news that she would not live or at the very least would be severely brain damaged. We called the church during the meeting to ask them to pray. Pastor Norcross called a deacon to come and to lead in prayer while he and his wife and daughter came to lay hands on Martha. The little crib shook as we prayed, then pastor went back to the service to tell them he knew Martha was healed. Two days later she began to eat and to talk. Six weeks later she was discharged, perfectly normal. PRAISE GOD! It made me think of the shepherd who left the ninety and nine to go after the one that was lost.[95]

Upon completion of their fifteen years of pastoring in Sarnia, Pastor and Mrs. Norcross moved to pastor in Youngstown, Ohio, and Rev. Jim Routley, a son of A. O. Routley, served Bethel as the interim pastor.

245 Essex Street today. It is now a Masonic Lodge.

An artist's sketch of Robert Norcross, Sr.

6

Bethel Pentecostal Church at 1565 London Line

In 1968, Rev. Tom and Eileen Richardson came to pastor the church. It was Pastor Richardson who encouraged the church to buy a property on London Road (now London Line), where Bethel Pentecostal Church exists today. It was approximately ten acres, and was purchased for $42,500.00. During the Richardsons' eleven years of ministry at the Essex Street location in Sarnia, the church implemented a bus ministry, contributed to the planting of new churches through the PAOC's "Penny Fund," renovated the Essex Street site, paid off the church mortgage, and saw the Sunday School grow to about four hundred children.

*Tom & Eileen
Richardson
served as
pastors at
Bethel from
1968-1978.*

At one time during his ministry in Sarnia, Pastor Richardson miraculously escaped a fire that had fully engulfed a trailer he was in.

While he was hospitalized for severe burns to his hands and face, the church Board assumed leadership of the services. During his latter years in Sarnia, Pastor Richardson wanted to build a new church on Bethel's newly purchased property, but the congregation was not ready to do so. One testimony from a lady named Donna who attended the church during this time attests to the continuing faith and powerful prayer of the leadership of Bethel:

> I have lived in Sarnia for many years and had attended Bethel Church while Tom Richardson was pastor. His faith was simple and powerful. My father was dying as a result of open heart surgery, his renal artery disintegrated and could not be attached to the heart/lung machine. The doctors said that the poisons from his kidneys had entered his bloodstream and he could not survive. I went to Pastor Richardson for prayer. His faith was simple; a 30 second prayer, and my father walked out of the hospital in a few days.[96]

Rev. George and Ruby Carroll came to Sarnia on October 1, 1978. The Essex Street church had reached its capacity, and it was time to move. Pastor Carroll immediately focussed the church towards work on the London Road site with a projected cost of $950,000. Ab Gingrich was the contractor for the project, and the church building was completed in November 1980.[97] It featured a sanctuary with a seating capacity of between six and seven hundred people. The rest of the building was devoted to the purposes of Christian Education,[98] as the Sunday School and related programs for children and youth had become a dominant ministry of the church. *The Sarnia Observer* reported at the time that "included in the plans is the construction of an educational wing accommodating 600 to 800 students for the learning of Christian education, with the Bible being the main text."[99]

In the 1980's, many Pentecostal churches began hiring specialized ministers, such as those serving specifically in music and youth ministry. Bethel was no exception. Ken Powell was a Minister of Church Ministries, which ballooned to include over a dozen individual ministries. Jerry Fulham was the Minister of Music and the Youth Pastor.

When Fulham left, Grant Hick became the Minister of Music, and Paul Carroll became the Youth and "College and Careers" Pastor. Church ministries abounded for all age groups in the new building. The King's Kids Nursery School, a cooperative nursery school that still exists as a separate entity from the church, also began during this time, specifically in 1981. Sunday attendance at the church was at an all-time high, with a weekly attendance that was well more than double that of Bethel's previous Essex Street location. In 1985, Rev. and Mrs. Carroll left to pastor the Pentecostal church in Windsor.

George & Ruby Carroll in the 1980's.

Rev. William and Sheila Morrow came to the church immediately following, and served the church for five years. Pastor Morrow was a public school teacher for two years before attending Eastern Pentecostal Bible College to become a pastor. Prior to arriving in Sarnia, he pastored in Montreal, Quebec, and Smiths Falls, Ontario. By the time he came to Bethel in 1985, he had completed two college diplomas, an undergraduate degree in history, a master's degree in counselling, and had taught at Eastern Pentecostal Bible College for five years.[100] Writing in 1996, Pastor Morrow recounts, "In 1985 I returned to pastoring, this time in Sarnia, Ontario, where [at] a large vibrant church … I had the privilege to work with the finest pastoral staff and lay leadership I have ever known."[101] The pastoral staff Pastor Morrow refers to was Grant Hick, who continued in his role as music minister until 1987, Todd Manuel, who assumed the duty of ministering to youth and young adults, and frequently led worship, Ken Powell, who continued to function very well in his church ministries role, Charlie Routley, a long-time lay leader who was given an official place on staff as minister of visitation, and in 1988, the addition of Les Paulsen as associate pastor. Pastor Morrow focussed on debt reduction for the cost of the new church building. He also spearheaded the construction of Bethel Manor, a fifty-unit apartment building for seniors established by the church on the property immediately to the east of the church at 1575 London Line. The church grew to the point where in September of 1989, it became necessary to hold two Sunday morning services to accommodate everybody.

William Morrow, pictured here during his time as the General Superintendent of the Pentecostal Assemblies of Canada.

Thirty kilometres downriver, Courtright Pentecostal Church, which had been established in 1957, decided to move eight kilometres north to the more populated Corunna in 1988.[102] With the cooperation of Pastor Morrow and the Western Ontario District of the PAOC, Pastor David Rutledge helped to transplant what is now Parkway Pentecostal Church in Corunna. This church met in the local Catholic elementary school on Sunday mornings, but joined with Bethel for Sunday evening services until their own facility was completed in 1989.[103]

In 1990, Pastor Morrow left Bethel to serve as the District Superintendent of the Western Ontario District of the PAOC, where he served faithfully and effectively for six years. He was then nominated to serve at the national level, where from 1997-2008 he served as the General Superintendent of the PAOC with excellence, making it his priority to restructure the PAOC International Office leadership and staff. Although he had intended to retire after this, he was asked to serve as the President of the PAOC's Master's College and Seminary, which he did from 2008-2013. In each of these posts, Pastor Morrow helped to bring financial stability—debt reduction and sound financial strategies—to the corresponding organizations, something he had successfully accomplished at Bethel in Sarnia. Also, early in 1990, Ken Powell left Bethel to assume a leadership position in the Christian Education Department of the Western Ontario District of the PAOC.

Rev. Bert and Shirley Liira came to Bethel from pastoring in the Ottawa area in 1990. Soon after, their son-in-law, Steve Moore, came on staff as the Children's Education Pastor, accompanied by his wife, Lori. Pastor Liira believed that the family of God should be involved in working hard for the Lord and encouraged everyone to participate in the mission of the church. During this time at Bethel there continued to be a strong emphasis on Children's and Bus Ministries. Sunday School for all ages continued during the first service, and Children's Church for kids up to Grade 6 was held in the gymnasium during the second service.

Shirley Liira, a former schoolteacher and the daughter of PAOC pastor Ross Schwindt, was the Minister of Music and led thriving choirs for both adults and children. In fact, in 1990, there were six choirs with a total enrollment of over two hundred people: the primary choir, the junior choir, the intermediate choir, the youth chorale, the adult choir, and the senior's choir.[104] Each Christmas and Easter, she wrote and produced an original cantata. There was enthusiastic participation from the congregation, with each production involving over a hundred people. Many from the community came to see these musical performances, and whole families were brought into the kingdom through the presentation of the gospel in music. Pastor Liira recalls, "The congregation at Sarnia Bethel was very faithful, very loyal, and very enthusiastic. They loved God and they loved to be involved, and it was just a joy to see that they came to church enthusiastically and not reluctantly."[105]

*For its first thirty years on London Line, Bethel Pentecostal
Church's décor was green, including its carpet, pew cushions,
platform curtain, and a green edition of the Pentecostal
hymnbook, "Hymns of Glorious Praise."*

During this time, the church raised significant funds for an addition to the church which was never realized, and would instead be applied towards the church mortgage. Other pastoral staff assisted in various roles: Les and Lois Paulsen were the associate pastors, and John and Beverlie Stewart were the youth pastors. Charlie and Cora Routley continued to be the visitation pastors, and later, after Cora's death,

Charlie continued to minister with his second wife, Aileen, delivering the full gospel message to seniors that "Jesus alone is the Saviour, Healer, Baptizer and soon coming King. "[106] Randy and Amanda Raycroft joined the pastoral team as youth pastor when the Stewarts left this position after three years of service in 1994. Then, in 1995, the Liiras and the Moores left to pastor in British Columbia.[107]

Bert & Shirley Liira, pictured here in 1992.

In April of 1996, Rev. Gary and Pamela Nettleship assumed leadership at Bethel. Prior to becoming a pastor, he had worked in a medicinal research lab, and as a national Canadian sales manager for a multinational science laboratory instrument company. Turning from these jobs to pursue God's leading in pastoral ministry, he pastored three churches before his arrival at Sarnia. Like many before him, Pastor Nettleship had a heart for revival,[108] and a desire to see the church passionately pursuing God. In 1997, the Holy Spirit moved in an intense way at Bethel. Many people were healed and saved. Pastor Nettleship encouraged the church to practice the spiritual discipline of prayer and fasting. Around this time, he attended the Brownsville Revival in Pensacola, Florida, and invited Rev. John Kilpatrick to visit Bethel. Although Kilpatrick did not end up coming to Sarnia, numerous other guests did in 1997, including Moses Vegh, Judy Buffum, Rev. Carey Robertson, Rev. Paul Schoch, evangelist Steve Oosthuyzen, evangelist Michael Livengood, and evangelist Bob Winter. The church's emphasis shifted from one of full participation in church programs to praying and longing for personal and corporate spiritual revival.

Gary & Pamela Nettleship pastored at Bethel
from 1996 to 2004.

Bethel hosted a mortgage burning ceremony on January 31, 1999, having paid off all its debts. In April 1999, the church hired Pastor Joe Manafo as the Youth Pastor. Later that year, Pastor Dan Helps, who attended Bethel with his family, responded to the church's desire to plant a church in Bright's Grove, a suburb of Sarnia about 12 km away from Bethel. It was a growing community and had very few churches considering the size of its population. On September 19, 1999, Lakeshore Community Church began services in the local school, and later constructed a beautiful facility on a property that overlooks Lake Huron and the Bright's Grove beach. This church now has its own history of God's work in their midst, and Rev. Troy Toby is the pastor.

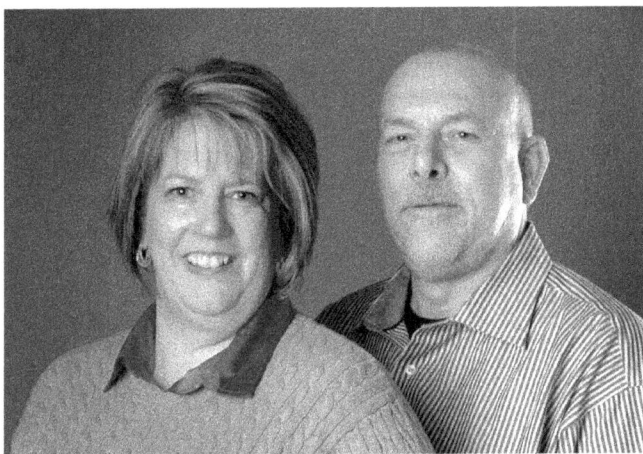

In 1999, Dan and Patti Helps led a team from Bethel
Pentecostal Church to plant Lakeshore Community Church
in Bright's Grove, a bedroom community in Sarnia.

In 2000, Rev. Tim and Kim Gibb came to Bethel as associate
pastors. Although not specifically music pastors, they were quite musical.
Pastor Gibb loved leading worship and the church very much enjoyed
Kim's singing. In 2001, the church hired Sue Spinks as the Children's
Pastor. In February 2004, Pastor Nettleship left to lead Trinity
Pentecostal Church in Oshawa. Sue Spinks left Bethel around this time as
well. Upon Pastor Nettleship's resignation, the church board approached
Pastor Gibb to assume the vacant senior leadership role of the church.

In April of 2004, Pastor Gibb became Bethel's youngest lead
pastor at 34 years of age. Pastor Tim and Kim Gibb were both graduates
of Zion Bible College, Barrington, Rhode Island (now called Northpoint
Bible College, Haverhill, Massachusetts). He quickly focused the church
towards missions and local outreach. In its history, Bethel has never
given more to missions than under Pastor Gibb's leadership. His
preaching style was of the old-time Pentecostal style—loud, boisterous,
and passionate. He had previously pastored in Woodstock, Ontario and

Brandon, Manitoba. His father, Rev. Robert Gibb, was a compassionate and caring pastor of many years in Montreal, Quebec. His mother, Margaret, was also well-known in the PAOC, having spoken at various sessions at its national General Conference.[109] She was recognized as being an articulate and thoughtful advocate for the recognized role of women in ministry in the PAOC.[110]

Tim & Kim Gibb, pictured here in the early 2000's

With the absence of a Children's Pastor, one of the first things Pastor Gibb did in his new role was to appoint a sub-committee to hire a new Children's Pastor, suggesting his younger sister, Tricia Gibb, as a candidate. She was hired initially for a summer, and was then brought on staff as the full-time Children's Pastor. Soon after, the church also hired Gianpaolo and Alicia Galessiere as the Youth Pastors.

In 2005, Pastor Gibb lead his first missions team from Bethel to Uganda for ministry in churches and at pastors' conferences. The church provided 300 Bibles and 100 bicycles to Ugandan pastors. Bethel would return with teams to the continent of Africa in 2006, 2007, 2011, 2012, &

2014. One such trip included a gift of over $25,000 in medical equipment, accompanied by four nurses on the missions team. The year 2005 also marked twenty-five years of ministry on London Line, and several of Bethel's former pastors came to a special commemorative banquet. This same year, at Pastor Gibb's request, Caleb and Stephanie Courtney, both local public school teachers, assumed volunteer leadership of the Music Ministry, just in time for what would become known as the Sarnia Revival.

Pastor Tim Gibb presenting a Ugandan pastor with a brand new bright yellow bicycle in 2005.

7

The Sarnia Revival

Pastor Gibb regularly invited evangelists and missionaries to speak at Bethel. On April 7, 2004, evangelist Ted Shuttlesworth, Sr., came to Bethel and declared to the congregation, "And I prophesy to you that there shall be longer meetings come back into the church, and it shall not be one night or two nights, but it shall be weeks upon weeks."[111] The following year during another visit to the church, he prophesied that there would be "some building, and some remodeling, and some expansion"—something that had only just been discussed among the church board. He continued to prophesy about revival, that "people would come from near and far ... and wonderful miracles will take place."[112] On the first weekend in December, Dr. Tom Renfro and his wife, Sid, came to speak to Bethel. A medical doctor, he had experienced miraculous healing from cancer. Having heard his testimony on the Christian Broadcasting Network's television program *The 700 Club*, Pastor Gibb invited him to share it in Sarnia at some special meetings. These meetings prepared the church for what would be a crazy and amazing experience of God's miraculous presence within the coming year.

In March 2006, Pastor Gibb called the church to a twenty-one day fast. During the fast, evangelist Reva Kasey came from Kentucky to Sarnia for a couple of meetings. Extended prayer meetings were added to the church schedule during the fast, each Tuesday morning and Friday night. The fast was scheduled to end on Easter Sunday morning, and it was a glorious morning of worship. Brian Warren, a former pro football player turned pastor, spoke to a crowd of about 400 people in the evening service on Easter Sunday. On April 26, 2006, evangelist Tom Scarrella from Fort Lauderdale, Florida, came to Sarnia to host a one-night meeting. In this meeting, several healings occurred. A boy named Keith, who was legally blind received full sight. A man named Steve was healed of total deafness in his one ear. In light of these things, Pastor Gibb made the spontaneous decision to hold another meeting the next night. In a commemorative memoir on the tenth anniversary of "The Sarnia Revival," Pastor Gibb wrote:

> 2006 will long be remembered as a year when God moved in a special way with miraculous signs and wonders. […] It was a season that was initiated by the prophetic word and the glory of God. The result of the revival was that hundreds of lives were powerfully touched by God, many receiving physical healings and salvation, and many were baptized in the Holy Spirit. It is the story of a Pentecostal church in a small city in Ontario, Canada, that pressed into a move of God which resulted in 116 consecutive services over 20 weeks and saw people travel from 15 U.S. States and 7 Canadian Provinces to attend revival services. The revival was eventually told around the world through the television programs 100 Huntley St. and The 700 Club, through the Evangelical Fellowship of Canada, and in printed page in the 2006 September edition of Charisma magazine.[113]

The nightly services usually featured a full time of worship, with attendance fluctuating anywhere from 80 to 600 people, depending on the service. Services began at 7:00 PM, and would last several hours, sometimes reaching into the late hours of the night. Pastor Gibb hired Pastor Greg Holmes as an associate pastor primarily to assist with these meetings, as well as with local outreach, and Pastor Holmes would often begin meetings recounting the miracles that had happened in the previous evening's service. Although exuberant worship and passionate preaching were a scheduled part of these services, some services were spontaneously devoted to loud corporate prayer, while others were spontaneously quiet and contemplative towards the Lord with a deeply penetrating sense of his presence.

There are too many stories of miraculous healing to record here. In the month of May 2006 alone, there were more than 100 reported miracles. Pastor Gibb remembers three times where ambulances brought the sick to revival services for healing. A local teenager held a healing meeting on his high school's front lawn one day, and about a hundred students gathered to watch. This student made the front page of local newspapers and was the talk of local radio shows because he was suspended for drawing such a large, uncontrolled crowd near the school.[114] Visiting evangelists and preachers included Tom Scarrella, Reva Kasey, Sue Curran, Brian Warren, Faytene Kryskow (now Faytene Grasseschi), Mike Kerychuk, Ken Bombay, Mark Davy, and Sid Roth. Songwriter and worship leader Allen Froese was a frequent visitor as well. The nightly services came to a natural close in August of 2006.

One of many services during the Sarnia Revival of 2006.
Passionate worshippers often filled the altar area at the front
of Bethel's auditorium, singing loudly, with arms raised high
to the Lord.

Let Revival Fire Fall
ALLEN FROESE

KEY of (D)

D   G   Bm7   A   Asus4   Em7   G2

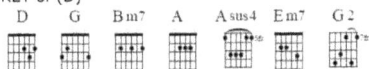

Verse 1:
```
D       G       Bm7       A
Fan into flame the fire of our first love
D       G    Bm7          A
Let us remain passionate for You
D       G       Bm7        A
Touch us again with power from You God
D/F#    G         Bm7          A
We can't contain our longings for You
        G            Asus
Lord You hear when we call
```

Chorus:
```
D
Let revival fire fall
Em7
Let revival touch us all
Bm7     A      D/F#     G2
Holy Spirit You are welcome here
D
Let revival sweep this land
Em7
Let revival blaze again
Bm7     A      D/F# G2   D      Em      Bm   A  D/F#  G
Holy Spirit be forever near
```

Verse 2:
```
D             G   Bm7        A
You made us one joined by Your Sprit
D        G     Bm7               A
Our sins are gone through Your blood most high
D             G     Bm7      A
Lord You have won the battle forever
D/F#    G       Bm7          A
Satan is done condemned for all time
        G         Asus
All You are we desire
```

Bridge:
```
        Em7                 D/F#
Let the blind eyes see, let the deaf ears hear
        G2              Asus  A
Let the dead ones live again
        Em7                 D/F#
Set the captives free, mend the broken hearts
        G2              Asus  A
Let Your Word spread on the earth
```

© 2006 Allen Froese

---

*Allen Froese wrote "Let Revival Fire Fall" out of his own
experience with the Sarnia Revival in 2006. It appeared on
his album* Faith Inside, *which was released in 2011.*

8

Modern History (2007-2016)

On September 3, 2007, Pastors Keith and Patricia Patrick arrived in Sarnia, and became Associate Pastors, remaining so to this day. Together this couple ministers primarily in areas of teaching, visitation, prayer, discipleship, and spiritual formation. Originally from the United Kingdom, and having served together in the Royal Air Force, they left their home to become a part of the Brownsville Revival in the year 2000, and subsequently moved to Sarnia to be closer to family. They came to Bethel, attracted by the church's hunger to see the Spirit of God move in spontaneous, miraculous ways. Many people have discovered their spiritual gifts, found spiritual freedom, and have been baptized in the Holy Spirit with speaking in tongues, through the Patricks' faithful ministry at Bethel.

Keith and Patricia Patrick, pictured here in 2014.

In 2009, at a cost of 1.7 million dollars, Bethel completely renovated the main floor of the church, updating its 30-year-old décor and upgrading the technology used throughout the church, including in its Sunday services. It included an expansion to the east side of the building to make room for more office space, and allowed the nursery to move closer to the sanctuary, rather than stay at the far end of the building. A café was included in the plans, as well as an outdoor patio. While the addition also added room upstairs, this was left unfinished to avoid an undue burden of debt. While the sanctuary was being renovated during the month of January in 2010, Bethel met at Sarnia Collegiate Institute and Technical School (SCITS), using the school's auditorium for regular Sunday services, and various classrooms for children's ministry. Bethel held their grand opening celebration in April 2010, with Mayor Mike Bradley, Pastor George Carroll, and Ab Gingrich in attendance.

Chris Guerette, a board member and the chairman of the renovation committee, speaks to the congregation at the grand opening. The church board, building contractors, city officials, and dignitaries are standing behind him.

The congregation in Sunday worship on the day of Bethel's grand opening celebration in April 2010, after major renovations.

In January of 2011, the church hired a full-time communications director, Jordan Ouellette. A recent high school graduate who completed his co-op at the church, he gave the church a consistent and professional public presentation in video, graphic design, media, and many of its other creative endeavours. He left the church in 2015 to design for a major Canadian e-commerce company in Ottawa, and Pastor Gibb's son, Cayden, stepped into this role shortly thereafter. Assisting Pastor Tricia part time in children's ministry in 2011 were Kim Lapier, Mary Elliot (now Mary Carruthers), and Kim Gibb. Bethel hosted Richard Crisco for three nights of special "Encounter Services" in January, and featured regular live streaming of The Bay of the Holy Spirit (Alabama) Revival services with Rev. John Kilpatrick and evangelist Nathan Morris. Special guests in 2011 included David Mainse of 100 Huntley Street, former Bethel pastor Lyndon Stratton, missionary Steve Hawkins, evangelist Dr. Larry Martin, missionary Mike Kerychuk, missionary Mark Griffin, Glen Rutledge of 100 Huntley Street, itinerant speaker Joanne Goodwin, evangelist John Wilkinson, evangelist Dominic Galati, Jr., Dr. John Tweedie of Christians for Israel Canada, missionary Ray Bradbury, singer-songwriters Rich and Lavinia Celaire, evangelist Mark Davy, and former Bethel pastor Gary Nettleship. Over the decades, many teams from Bethel have engaged in short-term overseas mission trips. In 2011, Pastor Tricia went on a mission trip to Thailand, and Pastor Gibb led a team from Bethel to Kenya and Uganda.

In 2012, Bethel embarked on a unique one-year series of messages that worked through the Bible in an entire year. This series, called "The Story," invited every age group and every person to participate by reading through the Bible at the same pace. Each Sunday would feature a message selected around one of the week's readings. This was also true of stories told in children's ministry and messages at youth meetings. The series went from January 8 to November 25, with only a few adjustments around special holidays. Special speakers over the year included missionary Don Mann, evangelist John Wilkinson, PAOC General Superintendent David Wells, evangelist Michael Livengood, pastor Phillip Corbett from Texas, and David Hessler of Walk Thru the Bible. Also in 2012, Bethel sent a missions team to Ukraine to run a VBS program at a government-run orphan camp with six hundred children, at the Ukrainian government's invitation. In partnership with the Ukraine Bible Society, every orphan received a Bible, and nearly five hundred of the children asked to receive Christ into their lives.

In 2013, Bethel hosted renowned missionary to India, Huldah Buntain. It is interesting to note that approximately seventy years earlier, her husband Mark had been a visiting evangelist in Sarnia, in the early days of the Sarnia church. For the first time in several years, the church also hosted the dramatic presentation *Heaven's Gates and Hell's Flames* over a weekend. This was followed immediately by the *Alpha Course*, a course designed to introduce people to the basics of the Christian faith. The church had "Encounter Services" with evangelist John Wilkinson in the spring, and evangelist Ted Shuttlesworth in the fall. Pastor Gibb's mother, Margaret Gibb, spoke to the church on Mother's Day and was ordained later that year on October 20, 2013. Missionary Ed Dickson

spoke in June, shortly after Bethel had raised funds to purchase a
property and to construct the very first evangelical church building in
Smila, Ukraine.

*The first evangelical church building in Smila, Ukraine, one
of Bethel's missionary endeavours in 2013.*

Bethel also decided, as a part of its missionary efforts, to provide
wages for a young lady named Lena Taran to lead Bible Kids Clubs in
Orphanages in Krivvy Rog, Ukraine. Missions giving in 2013 reached a
record high of $217,588—more than twice the budgeted amount of
$100,000. Missionaries Don Mann and Ray Bradbury, evangelist Nathan
Morris, and worship leader Lydia Stanley Marrow were among those who
ministered to Bethel over the course of the year.

In 2014, Family Fun Day, an annual community event organized,
hosted, and run by Bethel, drew over twenty-eight hundred people from
the community onto the church property, and required 160 volunteers
from the church. This event, first held in 2007, has continued to grow
every year, and is funded largely through partnerships with local
businesses. In November of 2014, Lydia Stanley Marrow, who was called
to music ministry at the Brownsville Revival, recorded a live album at
Bethel. It was produced by Lindell Cooley. Marrow has preached and led

worship at Bethel several times over the years, and consistently commends the Sarnia congregation for their heart of worship, saying, "I travel to a lot of churches, and let me tell you, y'all know how to worship!" This recording of worship at Bethel has since gone around the world. Evangelist Nathan Morris, and missionaries Ed Dickson and Huldah Buntain were among the guest speakers in 2014.

A promotional image from Shake the Nations, the evangelistic ministry of Nathan Morris, for an album, Forevermore, recorded live at Bethel by Lydia Marrow and produced by Lindell Cooley. It was released in late 2015.

In May of 2015, Bethel began to raise funds for the renovation of the children's ministry area in the upper level of the church, and to finish the unused portion of space from the 2009 renovation project. This part of the church had not been significantly updated in over thirty years, and it wore its age. The project called for improved access, including new stairs, and elevator, and appropriately child-sized bathrooms. The church board challenged the congregation to raise a million dollars, leading the giving by example. The million-dollar goal would both finish the project and bring the existing mortgage down to under a million dollars. The fundraising project, called Building Our Future, is still in progress. In eighteen months, Bethel has raised over $500,000 in addition to its regular operating expenses and mortgage payments, while maintaining a positive cash balance in the bank. Missions giving continues to be over $100,000 annually.

Bethel enjoyed the ministry of several guests in 2015. Rodney Howard-Browne held a "Great Awakening" week of meetings at the church. He brought with him his associate pastor, Eric Gonyon, and twenty students from his Bible school, the River Bible Institute in Tampa, Florida. During the day, the students joined with those from Bethel to engage in evangelism throughout the city of Sarnia. Other visiting guests over the year included Jan Painter, Tracy Stewart, Huldah Buntain (now 91 years of age), Caroline Barnett, and Russ Taff.

This brings our history to 2016.[115] Bethel continues to participate in missions by supporting missionaries and participating in short-term missions trips. The church continues to experience miracles, like that of Andrea, who was extraordinarily healed of blindness in a meeting with evangelist Ted Shuttlesworth. Bethel continues to be a church of all ages, and as members remember those who have passed on, they also celebrate new children being born and dedicated to the Lord.

The story of Bethel Pentecostal Church continues to be written. For over a decade now, Pastor Gibb has given leadership to the Lord's work in and through Bethel Pentecostal Church. In February of 2011, Pastor Gibb wrote an article entitled "Atmospheres, Climates, and Cultures,"[116] describing Bethel as forward thinking, next generation minded, participatory, a place of unconditional love and acceptance (which allows for loving correction), orderly, excellent, expecting the signs and wonders of Scripture, full of integrity, generous, consisting of ministering members, valuing the preaching of the word of God, embracing the power and necessity of prayer, and possessing missionary zeal. This describes a truly Pentecostal church.

Just as Barbara Johnston was baptized in the Spirit and became a ministering member in Sarnia, and then a missionary to India, so members of Bethel today become ministers and missionaries in their communities, open to God's direction in their lives. Just as Edna Riblet was baptized in the Spirit and began preaching that Jesus was the Saviour, Baptizer in the Spirit, Healer, and Soon Coming King, so too can the members of Bethel testify to these things today. Many have experienced this salvation, this Spirit baptism, and healing. Many anticipate the imminent second coming of Jesus for his church. In the meantime, the people of Bethel seek the presence of God in their lives and in their church, knowing that he has sent his Holy Spirit and is empowering them to accomplish his mission on earth. Pastor Gibb continues to be passionate about revival and missions, and often travels to minister as a teacher, evangelist, and missionary, doing so sometimes as a part of Bethel's endeavours, but also on his own vacation time.

The year 2016 marks eighty years since Edna Riblet began a Sunday School under a hawthorn tree on White Street in Sarnia. While these years testify to God's faithfulness and goodness, Bethel always looks to the future expecting even "greater things than these" until the Lord returns. It is fitting to end with a poem by Charlie Routley, who was a longstanding volunteer leader and lay pastor for many years at Bethel, and passed into eternity earlier this year at the age of ninety-six.[117] The poem is simply entitled, "Commitment."

> To all who are members of Christ's church
> There's a work for you to do.
> You're the only one who can heed the call
> The Master is counting on you.
>
> In one great church of our modern age,
> The vision they've caught – not a few
> On the ship of the church are no passengers
> All are members of the crew.
>
> To put it again in another way
> Christ has redeemed a great team by His grace
> None are asked to be mere spectators
> All are runners in this holy race.
>
> Don't forget why He has called you.
> Don't forget that you are His.
> His image He'll stamp on your life, child,
> His will is the best – so don't miss.

May each person who calls Bethel their home know that they are a crucial part of carrying out the mission of God in Sarnia and around the world.

Bethel Pentecostal Church, pictured here in the winter.

Bethel's logo since 2006.

Asides

THE WORD "MISSION" AS "CHURCH"

Preeminent scholar of the Azusa Street Revival, Cecil M. Robeck, writes:

> The use of the term 'mission' to describe a local congregation is relatively uncommon outside the holiness and Pentecostal movements. Among the more radical elements of the holiness movement in the late nineteenth century, the term frequently described works that were independent of denominational control—typically small, storefront congregations led by some charismatic figure. Many of these 'missions' offered what is commonly called 'compassionate ministry.' They commonly served the poor, women, alcoholics and drug addicts, prostitutes and others marginalized by society. These missions often offered not only spiritual help, but also material aid. Early Pentecostals such as Charles F. Parham ... expanded the meaning of this term beyond the local level by using it as a part of their denominational names [such as] the Apostolic Faith Mission (Baxter Springs, Kansas).[118]

THE FOURFOLD OR "FULL" GOSPEL

After attending Braeside Camp in 1938, Edna Riblet returned to Sarnia preaching the "Full Gospel." In the history of Braeside Camp, the authors write that at Braeside in the 1930's:

Four great Bible truths were boldly proclaimed with continued emphasis: The need for sinful man to be "born again" through repentance from sin and personal faith in the Lord Jesus Christ; the experience of the Baptism in the Holy Ghost with the evidence of speaking in other tongues as on the day of Pentecost; they fearlessly and effectively heralded their faith in Divine Healing, asserting "Jesus Christ is the same, yesterday and today and forever" (Hebrews 13:8). They preached with great conviction the imminent return of Christ for His Church and lived in momentary expectancy of the Lord's promise "I will come again."[119]

Perhaps the most succinct published statement of the Fourfold Gospel came from Aimee Semple McPherson. She was an internationally renowned evangelist in the 1920's who was born in Salford, Ontario (near Ingersoll), held tent meetings across the North American continent, and finally settled into pastoring Angelus Temple, a church she built which accommodated crowds of over 5000 every Sunday in Los Angeles. She wrote:

Jesus saves us according to John 3:16. He baptizes us with the Holy Spirit according to Acts 2:4. He heals our bodies according to James 5:14-15. And Jesus is coming again to receive us unto Himself according to 1 Thessalonians 4:16-17.[120]

In his landmark 1987 study on Pentecostal theology, entitled *Theological Roots of Pentecostalism*, Wesleyan scholar Donald W. Dayton describes these four themes of the fourfold gospel as "well nigh universal within the [Pentecostal] movement, appearing ... in all branches and varieties of Pentecostalism."[121] While Pentecostal services may look or feel different from place to place, these themes—salvation, Spirit baptism, healing, and Jesus' imminent return for his church—characterize the typical emphases of Pentecostal theology the world over.

LAY MINISTRY

Although this book focusses specifically on the role of each Senior Pastor, it is abundantly clear to the author that there are literally hundreds of people who have led and participated in the ministry of the Bethel Pentecostal Church in Sarnia over the years. Each of these people has an accompanying testimony of God's work in their life. Many have understood that their work has eternal significance. Bethel would not exist as it does today except for those members who have believed they have been called by God to minister to others.

The "laity" has traditionally been defined as "those in the Christian faith who are not the clergy." To early Pentecostals, who believed that every believer was a missionary, and thus, a minister, such a division between these terms would be problematic. To them, if someone is a believer, they are also a minister. Historically, Pentecostals never left the work of the ministry to a paid staff member, such as a pastor. All hands were needed on deck in these, the last days. They adopted the philosophy of John Wesley, the father of Methodism, who believed that believers with no formal academic training, but a legitimate call of God, could be effective ministers of the Gospel.

Each member of the early Pentecostal church liberally gave of their time, money, and resources to accomplish the work of the ministry. This began with giving money directly to missionaries so they could travel to foreign lands, but also with paying the rent for their meeting places, and being hospitable—sharing food around the family dinner table with those in need, even when there might not be much to share. Lay ministry involved these things, along with regular evangelistic work, prayer, and gathering together.

Suggested Additional Reading

The following books are suggested for additional related reading. Prices given are in Canadian dollars at the time of publication, and are subject to change at any time.

Authentically Pentecostal
by Van Johnson and David Wells
100 pages, $4.00
Pentecostal Assemblies of Canada, 2010
ISBN: 978-1894325332

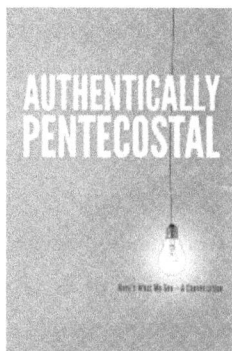

Pentecost: This Story is Our Story
by Robert Menzies
160 pages, $19.99
Gospel Publishing House, 2013
ISBN: 978-1607313410
Also available as an e-book.

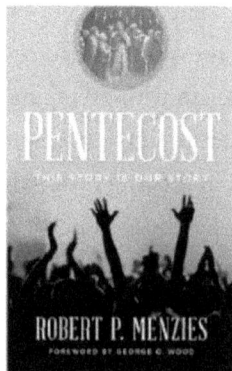

The Holy Spirit: A Pentecostal Perspective
by Anthony D. Palma
303 pages, $26.99
Gospel Publishing House, 2013
ISBN: 978-0882437866
Also available as an e-book.

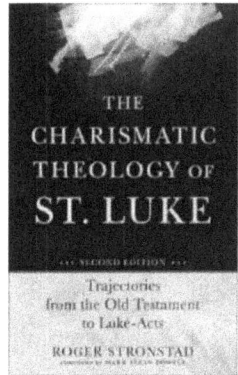

The Charismatic Theology of St. Luke
by Roger Stronstad
144 pages, $21.00
Baker Publishing Group, 2012
(originally published in 1984)
ISBN: 978-0801048586
Also available as an e-book.

*Canadian Pentecostals: A History of the
Pentecostal Assemblies of Canada*
by Thomas William Miller
450 pages, $17.99
Full Gospel Publishing House, 1994
ISBN: 1-895168-35-X

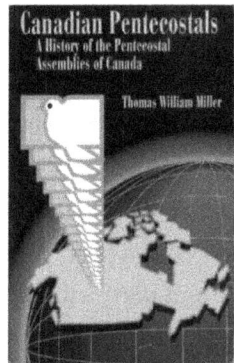

Addenda

HOW PENTECOST CAME TO TORONTO
(TORONTO, 1907)

The following is a reprint of Ellen Hebden's testimony as printed in
The Promise, *a newsletter distributed by their mission in Toronto. See*
Ellen Hebden, "How Pentecost Came To Toronto," The Promise *1, May*
1907: 1-3. Ellen Hebden held Pentecostal meetings in Sarnia in August of
1908.

On May 20th, 1906, we opened the Mission at 651 Queen Street East. The two upper flats of the building were at that time rented to other families at $33 per month. From the first we intended taking the whole building and opening it as a Faith Home. Therefore, after a short time, we gave all tenants notice to leave; and when they had all removed but two, we dedicated the place to God. It was a wonderful meeting, the spirit of prayer coming upon all present.

On Saturday, Nov. 17th, my husband had fasting and prayer, and that very night the last two tenants moved out of the building, and the peace of God filled the place. That same day I done quite a lot of visiting in connection with the mission, and, being very tired, I retired at 10:10 p.m. Only a short time elapsed when the Spirit of God prompted me to rise and pray, which I immediately did. For some months I had been seeking earnestly for more power to heal the sick, and with this desire still in my heart I began to pray. Suddenly the Holy Ghost fell upon me and I exclaimed aloud, "Oh Jesus! Thou art a real living person! Thou art lovely beyond description!" My whole being seemed to be filled with praise and adoration such as I had never realized before. The mighty power of God took possession of my hands, clasped them tightly together, and then moved them with such rapidity that it seemed as if they were severed from my arms.

I was praising Jesus all the time, and yet it did not appear to be me, but the power within that was praising Him. Then God began speaking to me. First, He said, "These are your hands no more." I exclaimed "Oh! thank you, Lord!" Again, my hands were raised by the power of God and pressed tightly into my right cheek; then they were moved to the left cheek and again pressed very hard. I said to the Lord, "What does this mean?" and a very quiet yet distinct voice said "Tongues." I said, "No, Lord, not Tongues." This time I felt afraid of grieving the Lord and I said, "Tongues, or anything that will please Thee and bring glory to Thy name." One unknown word was repeated several times and I thought that must be Tongues.

Suddenly a change came over me and I felt as if I were gently rising although I remained kneeling on the floor; and the Spirit said, "I will show you things to come." Just then a little fear crept into my heart and I said, "Lord, let my husband come." I tried to speak to my husband by failed, and I found that God wanted me to go through alone. Presently the power of God seemed to be lifted from me, and I returned to rest.

I awoke in the morning full of joy and gladness, knowing that I had received the Baptism of the Holy Ghost, and very eagerly I told my husband of my wonderful experience. He sat and listened, but it seemed to me that he did not understand what had taken place. He remarked quietly, "Well, you have had many wonderful experiences."

I thought within myself, "I shall wait and see what the Lord does." I had not long to wait; for that very morning, when we met together in the morning service at 10.45, as soon as I knelt in prayer, the

Holy Spirit manifested His power in such a wonderful manner that every one present saw that it was of God.

During the whole of that meeting the power of God was upon me. I spent the noon hour alone with God as the desire for food had entirely left me; God had laid a fast upon me. During the following days of fasting and prayer I felt stronger in my body that I had ever been any time previously in my life. In the afternoon of the same day I went down into the Mission intending to sit quietly on one side where I would not be seen. But God was having his way, and when the Holy Ghost again manifested His power, I could only cry out, "This is the power of the Holy Ghost! This is the power of the Holy Ghost!" Instead of the ordinary service we had a prayer meeting, when all present got down on their knees before God. That night I decided to remain upstairs, alone with God; and, as I was resting upon a couch, I again asked the Lord "what all this meant." The Spirit replied, "He was wounded for our transgressions, He was bruised for our iniquities; the chastisement of our peace was upon Him, and with His stripes we are healed."

Again God wonderfully manifested His power, for I felt that I was raised from the couch, and, without intending to do so, I hurried down to the night service, and took a seat at the front with my back to the people. As soon as I was seated, the speaker on the platform either read or quoted "He was wounded for our transgressions." The Spirit, through me, repeated these words after the speaker in such a loud voice that the people present declared that it did not sound like me speaking. This occurred after every sentence uttered by him finishing with "By His stripes we are healed."

I knew that the time had come when God wanted me to declare to the people what He had done. Stepping upon the platform, and realizing all the time that the power of God was upon me mightily, I testified to all that God had done for me, telling them how I had received the baptism of the Holy Ghost according to the Bible. After the testimony there followed a blessed season of prayer.

On Monday morning I arose again to spend the day with the Lord. I waited patiently for Him. At noon I took the word of God, read a portion of it and spread it upon the floor. I then knelt upon it and cried to the Lord to give me nothing only what corresponded with His word. Great peace filled my soul and I began to sing very quietly but to my amazement I was singing *in another language.* I said eagerly, "Is this Tongues?" and then another verse burst from my lips, and for two or three hours I sang in an unknown language: it was marvelous. I was afterwards told that the hall outside was filled with people listening to the singing.

About 7.30 p.m. a dear sister, who was at that time conducting a Bible Class on Monday nights, came into the room and kissed me. I exclaimed, "This is for the glory of God!" I did not think of attending the Bible Class that night; but, after a short time, I felt that same irresistible power moving me, and I arose quickly and hurried down to the Class. I went into the room just as the saints were rising from their knees, and suddenly the Spirit sang, through me, four verse in an unknown tongue. I saw tears come into the eyes of everyone present. After singing, I said again, "This is the power of the Holy Ghost." Then I left the meeting, and again the dear ones got down to pray. The Lord continued to speak through me at intervals. A week from the Wednesday following, as I knelt to pray, the Lord gave me another language that I could speak as fluently as if I had known it all my life. Later on the Lord gave me twenty-two languages, one night in a public meeting; and hundreds of verses of poetry have been given by the Spirit, also the interpretation of many. Sometimes the Lord gives me the interpretation of what others are saying; also I have been able to write all the languages that God has spoken through me, and many marvelous sketches have been drawn.

I give this testimony only for the glory of Jesus, who is so precious to me. The gift of Tongues was God's gift to me, and as such I value it, for everything which God bestows is good; but I shall never cease to praise him for the flood of love which filled my whole being and melted me into tenderness, and gave me such a yearning for souls as I had never had before.

A month later my husband received the baptism of the Holy Ghost and spoke in tongues.

The work has now been going on without a break for five months, between 70 and 80 having the baptism and the gift of tongues. Four workers have gone forth from this place to preach the Gospel and God is preparing others.

TESTIMONY OF
BARBARA JOHNSTON OF SARNIA
(INDIA, 1909)

The following is a reprint of Barbara Johnston's testimony as printed in a newsletter published by a mission in India. The daughter of John Johnston, who was a prominent principal and teacher in Sarnia at the time, Barbara had recently left for missions in India and married John Norton. See Mrs. John Norton, "Testimony" Jehovah-Jireh: A Witness to Christ's Faithfulness *1.4, December 1909.*

I was brought up in Christian home in Sarnia, Ontario, Canada. My mother gave me to the Lord at my birth. When I was about eight years old, two young out-going missionaries addressed our Sunday-School, and as they spoke of the needs of India my heart burned within me, and I said to myself, "Someday I hope I can go to India, to tell the people about Jesus." I was not converted till two years later, but that desire never left me. As I grew older it became a settled purpose, toward which all my plans tended. I thought I would study medicine, and

become a medical missionary, but a severe illness put an end to that plan.
I went to McMaster University, Toronto, in 1904, to prepare me for
whatever work the Lord had for me. At that time I was an earnest
struggling Christian, with a scarcely recognized longing for more than I
had known. Once at college I plunged into study with all my heart, and in
my desire to make the most of my opportunities I lost a good deal of my
zeal for the Lord's work. Early in 1906 I became thoroughly aroused to
the fact, that instead of becoming better fitted to serve the Lord, I was
losing what little earnestness I had had. At that time I made as full a
consecration of my life as I knew how, but I was not by any means
satisfied. My desire to work in India became stronger than ever, but I
began to feel how very unfit I was for a missionary.

In April 1907, my last year at college, I first heard of the Baptism
of the Holy Ghost, with the sign of speaking in new tongues, as it was
manifested in Toronto. I took my Bible, and hunted up everything I
could find on the Baptism of the Holy Ghost, and on speaking in
tongues, and I was convinced from the word, before attending any
meetings, that speaking in new tongues was the sign by which the
Apostles knew that the Holy Spirit had come. The speaking in tongues
was never much of a stumbling block to me. Six years before, in a Free
Methodist meeting, I heard the leader say of people, who I thought were
acting strangely, that they were full of the Holy Ghost as on the day of
Pentecost. I said then, "if they would speak with other tongues as they did
on the day of Pentecost I would believe they were filled with the Holy
Ghost." So when I met a people who did not speak in other tongues, I
was reminded of what I had said. I began to be hungry for the Baptism. I
was preparing for my final examination, but I was also seeking and
becoming increasingly hungry for the fullness. When at last I graduated
on May 15th, my degree seemed of little value compared with the blessing
I was seeking. The Lord had taken away all my pride in my learning or
ability to learn. I had even yielded to Him my desire to work for him in

India, and was content to toil humbly at home, if He wanted me to. The Lord also taught me about Divine Healing, of which I had known nothing, and in which I found many things to puzzle me. At first I was not willing to accept anything without a thorough examination, and that I did not think I had time for. But, after a time, I seemed to reach the place where the Lord could not do any more for me unless I would accept healing too. I had a real need of healing, so I just prayed and received the answer. "According to your faith be it into you," and I believed and was healed. Sanctification, also, was only a name to me. I had no clear idea of what it meant. Here again I tried to study and investigate, but had to fall back on faith, and one day I woke up to the fact that old habits and sins had lost their power over me.

After my graduation I still tarried on, learning lessons of faith and patience, and on May 29th, while praying, the Lord directed my attention to the two promises—"If ye then being evil know how to give good gifts to your children, how much more shall your heavenly father give the Holy Spirit to them that ask him." Luke 11:13, and also, "And this is the confidence which we have in him, that, if we ask anything according to his will, he heareth us; and if we know that he hears us whatsoever we ask, we know that we have the petitions that we desired of him." I John 5:14, 15. Quick as a flash, I saw "It must be according to his will because he has promised." I asked believing that I received, and the Lord's power was wonderfully manifested. After about two months waiting, I seemed to have reached the point where I could reach out and receive by faith. For the next two days I waited in quite expectancy for the Lord to manifest his presence according to his word. In the upper room, 651 Queen St. East, Toronto, on Friday afternoon, May 31st, the Lord came to me again in great power, and in the evening spoke through me in another tongue. Then I knew the work was finished. The Lord said to me "Go home to thy friends and tell them what great things the Lord has done for thee." I went home and tried to obey.

Just a little before I heard of Pentecost I had sent in an application to the Woman's Baptist Foreign Missionary Society, to be sent to India. I had passed the required medical examination and they were about to accept me. But when I began to seek Pentecost, I was afraid they might not approve, so I wrote and told them about it. They had heard little about it, and the matter was left over for a time, but I had never heard any more of the application. That was the hardest to give up. It was so easy to say "I'll go if you want me to go," but very hard to say "I'll stay at home if you want me there." But I said it, knowing that if the Lord wanted me in India, He could send me without any Board, but that idea was far from pleasant at first.

I took a country school near home, and taught there for a year, and the Lord was very near. How different was that year's teaching to any other I ever did! The school was large and rather troublesome, but the Lord bore the burdens, I didn't need to. All that year I had no word from the Lord about going to India. A little Pentecostal company had been gathered, and that seemed to be my care for the time. In August 1908 Mr. and Mrs. Hebden, from the Queen East Mission, where I had received the baptism, came to Sarnia to hold some meetings. It was just a few days before my school should start, and I was engaged there till the end of the year. One day I went around to the house where the Hebdens were staying, and found Mrs. Hebden lying on the couch, with closed eyes, talking in tongues such beautiful poetry. When I went in she was interpreting. She said "They are calling— They are calling to thee— They are calling from over the sea. The time of separation is coming for thee." Then came the word "India" and I knew it was for me. She went on "The Lord will open the way. Man closes up, but the Lord will open the way." I knew how true that was. Then she said again "The time of separation is coming for thee." When I asked her about it she said she had never known that India was the field to which I hoped to go, but that there was a lady, Mrs. Denney, speaking that very Sunday at the Queen East

Mission in Toronto, and that she was asking for workers for Ramabai's work. So I believed the Lord was calling me there. It did not seem for me to get away that fall. There was the mission, and there was the school. During my first week of the new term I prayed "Lord if you want me to go to India this fall, send someone to look after the mission." When I came home at the end of the first week, there was a man whom the Lord had sent to take charge of the Mission. Then I prayed "Lord send a teacher for my school." That was also provided, and in two weeks I was free to prepare to go to India. The money was provided, and I sailed Nov. 7th. How happy I was to be really on my way to the Land that I had thought of so long, and to know that God Himself was sending me there.

When I reached Ramabai's I found that she had been praying for the Lord to send someone to help her who knew Greek, and I seemed to be the answer to her prayer. After six months happy work at Mukti, the Lord me here to Dhond, just as surely as he first led me to India. I am still continuing Ramabai's work, and for the larger responsibilities that have fallen upon me, the Lord has given me the promise "My grace is sufficient for thee," and day by day I am proving it true. Praise His name. "He is faithful that promised."

EVANGELIST HELPS SAVE
SARNIA MAN FROM DROWNING
(SARNIA, 1938)

The following is a reprint (with permission) of an article printed in The Sarnia Canadian Observer *about a visiting Pentecostal Evangelist, Elwin Argue. See "Evangelist Helps Save Sarnia Man from Drowning,"* The Sarnia Canadian Observer, *Sarnia, Ontario, Monday, March 14, 1938, 3.*

Angler Fell Through Ice in Sarnia Bay—Evangelist Argue to Rescue—He and Companion Ventured Across Ice and Shivering Man Was Drawn to the Shore—

Evangelist Elwin Argue, of Winnipeg, who is conducting a soul-saving campaign in the Full Gospel Tabernacle here, was one of two men who, yesterday afternoon, rescued Joseph St. John, St. Vincent street, who fell through the ice of Sarnia Bay while fishing about 200 feet from shore. The other rescuer was V. Scully, of Montreal, who is visiting in the city. This was the first rescue from the St. Clair River this year.

By coincidence, Mr. Argue is a former lifeguard, who was stationed on Lake Winnipeg, and today he warned the public, particularly children that the ice in the bay is not safe.

Left Tackle Behind—

Mr. St. John, an employee of the Dominion Salt Company, apparently suffered no ill-effects, for he reported for work as usual last night. Shivering with cold the fisherman hurried home as soon as he was removed from the bay and left without taking his fishing equipment.

Mr. Argue was walking near the government warehouse at the harbor, where he heard calls for help. Looking in the direction from which they came he saw a man with only his arms and head above the ice.

"I ran quite a distance before I could get to him and when I got to the bank another man came up," the evangelist said. "We started out on the ice but when we couldn't reach him we had to get branches of trees which he grabbed, and we eventually were able to pull him out."

Mr. St. John's small son, who was with him, tried to help, but he was unsuccessful. Mr. Argue said the fisherman was nearly hysterical and he believed he had been in the water some minutes before being rescued. As soon as he was pulled safely to shore the man and the boy headed north along the railway tracks to home.

Employees of the Sarnia Elevator Company heard the shouts and summoned the fire department rescue squad, but in the meantime the man had been taken from the water.

Issues Warning—

Having almost gone through the ice while assisting in the rescue, Mr. Argue warned children against playing on the bay because the ice is too thin. In fact, he said, the ice is not thick enough in some spots, to hold even a child.

In conversation with a reporter for The Canadian Observer, Evangelist Argue said he was glad to have been of assistance during his visit to Sarnia.

SUNDAY SCHOOL IN WHAT IS KNOWN
AS SHANTY TOWN – SARNIA
(TORONTO, 1939)

The following is a reprint (with permission) of an article in The Pentecostal Testimony *about Edna Riblet's Sunday School meetings under the hawthorn tree. See "Sunday School in What is Known as Shanty Town – Sarnia,"* The Pentecostal Testimony *20.5, May 1, 1939, 11. According to maps published at the time, "Highway No. 7" is what is now known as London Road in Sarnia.*

SHANTY TOWN is a colony just outside Sarnia city limits— north of Highway No. 7—that grew up out of the depression. According to the local paper most of the inhabitants of this settlement are on relief rolls. Few have been self-sustaining for the past nine years. It is called Shanty Town because nearly all the homes are makeshift affairs.

Into this needy community came Mrs. Edna Riblet, whose husband had died over twenty years ago and who, having no children of her own, felt a call to do something for these children. She went through the streets and homes of Shanty Town and gathered thirteen children for her first service under a tree. The next Sunday she had forty-three children and she continued under that tree from August the 15th to October when a small house was donated for the work, an organ, stove, seats were also given and even a new floor. Today a fine spiritual work is being carried on in affiliation with the main Pentecostal Mission in Sarnia where Sister A. E. Stephan is Pastor.

LONG-TIME ORGANIST MARKS 60 YEARS
(SARNIA, 2016)

The following is a reprint (with permission) of an article printed in The Sarnia Observer *about organist Dorothy Dunne. See Paul Morden, "Long-Time Organist Marks 60 Years,"* The Sarnia Observer, *Sarnia, Ontario, Friday, February 5, 2016, A1-A2.*

It's 60 years and counting for Bethel Pentecostal Church organist Dorothy Dunne.

Dunne turns 88 this month, and during the service on Feb. 14, the Sarnia congregation is set to celebrate her six decades as its organist, although she doesn't think that's necessary. "I'm just doing something I really love to do," Dunne said. "Why make a big fuss about it?"

Pastor Tim Gibb said Dunne's contribution to the congregation goes beyond playing the organ at Sunday services. "She demonstrates an example for us of commitment, faithfulness," as well as a "real cheerfulness," and an ability to adjust to changing times and musical styles, he said. "She is a real blessing here, and the people just love her."

Dunne said that along with her ongoing enjoyment of playing the organ keeping her at her post, she's just following advice from the pulpit. Twice during the last 60 years, ministers paused during sermons to say, "You're a real blessing to this church, don't quit until the Lord tells you to quit," she said. One even added, "Don't let anybody tell you you're too old," Dunne said. "This was 20 years ago," she said. "I wasn't that old."

Born in Brantford, Dunne grew up in Owen Sound and Arthur in a musical family. Her sisters played guitar and violin, a brother played violin and their father played the spoons. "We played at dances, and political rallies, and stuff," she said. "Anything that needed some music."

When she was just three or four, Dunne remembers being set on pillows piled on a stool so she could reach the piano keys and play chords with the family band. She started piano lessons at age 11, and was playing at churches in Arthur a few years later. At age 19, she moved to Toronto to study music and began attending a Pentecostal church, where she played trumpet in its band. "That's where I met my husband," Dunne said.

Frank Dunne, who passed away in 1986, also played trumpet in the band and he noticed her the first time she came to rehearsal. "He said to the guy next to him, 'Who's that girl at the end of the line?'" Dunne said she and Frank began going out for coffee, and eventually married. They had the first of their eight children in Toronto, before Frank, a wireless operator for the government, was transferred to Sarnia in late 1955. "I told the Lord I wanted a good church to go to, and a ministry of some kind," Dunne said.

They attended Bethel Pentecostal, then on Essex Street, and she began playing organ for the congregation a few months later. The church later moved to London Line, and it has replaced the organ several times. But has Dunne stayed on.

There was a point in her life when it was a bit of a struggle, Dunne admits. That came during years she also worked nights at a nursing home, and would catch up her sleep on Sunday mornings, during the sermon. Dunne said that came to an end one Easter Sunday when the minister at the time was talking about how heaven awaited believers. "And then he said, 'Those that go to sleep will surely die,'" she said. "I came back to life in a hurry."

Dunne has an answer ready for a question about her favourite hymn. "I just enjoy playing whatever they're singing," she said. "But, I do like the old hymns." Although, she added, the new ones are "alright" too. "I used to play a lot of jazz when I was young, so these strange chords and rhythms … they come natural."

Looking ahead, Dunne said she's not thinking about retiring from playing at church. At the same time, she's open to what's ahead.

"I'm sure if I quit the organ, there would be something else for me to do," she said.

BETHEL PENTECOSTAL CHURCH CELEBRATES 80 YEARS (SARNIA, 2016)

The following is a reprint (with permission) of an article printed in The Sarnia Observer *about Bethel's 80ᵗʰ Anniversary in 2106. See Paul Morden, "Bethel Pentecostal Church Celebrates 80 Years,"* The Sarnia Observer, *Sarnia, Ontario, Saturday, November 12, 2016, A2.*

Bethel Pentecostal Church has grown since it began 80 years ago in Sarnia, while staying close to its roots.

Pastor Tim Gibb said the church that attracts more than 500 people to Sunday morning services on London Road, marked its 80th anniversary this year with a history written by Caleb Courtney, and video presentations shown to the congregation through September.

"It's a vibrant, multi-cultural congregation, well represented in every age category," Gibb said. "We have a growing nursery, children's ministry, youth ministry." The church is currently renovating the second storey of its building for its youth and children's ministry, Gibb said. "This is something we're really excited about, and it keeps with the original vision of Bethel Church," he said.

The church's story began in 1935 when Sarnia's Edna Riblet wanted to reach out to residents of a poor, south-end neighbourhood. She began offering games and activities for local children in a park, Gibb said. "What started out as outreach to children in the neighbourhood, turned into time for Bible study for adults and young people, and eventually became Bethel Pentecostal Church."

Its first home was in a donated house in the neighbourhood, and then it moved to a new building on Essex Street as the congregation grew.

It moved in 1980 to its current building at 1565 London Line. "I'm so pleased that we haven't lost the original DNA of this church," Gibb said. "The original DNA was outreach, reaching out to kids and young people, and an emphasis on the Holy Spirit, and the presence of God. "That is still very much a part of what we are, today."

One way the church continues to reach out to the community is through a Family Fun Day it has hosted for more than a decade. With the help of sponsors, 160 volunteers from the church plan a day of activities and fun each September, offered at no cost to families in the community. There are inflatables, a petting zoo, pony rides, a sports zone, a princess tea show, entertainment and a free barbecue. Last year, it rained on the day of event. "We still had 1,600 people come," Gibb said. "The year before that, we had 2,800. So, it's a big event." The Family Fun Day has grown so large the church arranges for parking at the Hiawatha Horse Park, with several buses running back and forth as a shuttle service. "We're already planning next year's," Gibb said. He has been at the church for 16 years, and has been its lead pastor for 12 years.

While the church has marked the milestone of its 80th anniversary, it has been looking to the future, he said. "We believe that this 80 years is just a foundation we're building upon for even greater things," Gibb said. "We've had just so many great people throughout the years who have really given their lives to see the work of the Lord go forward here."

Lists of Pastors,
Church Staff, and Board Members

PENTECOSTAL PASTORS IN SARNIA
BEFORE BETHEL PENTECOSTAL CHURCH

- Barbara Johnston, 1907-1908
- Unknown, 1908-1928
- Frank Jolley, 1929
- Unknown, 1929-1934
- Adeline Elizabeth Stephan, 1934-1948

BETHEL PENTECOSTAL CHURCH: SENIOR PASTORS

- Edna Riblet (née Gibson, later Hammond by 2nd marriage), 1936-1941
- A. O. & Lydia Routley, 1941-1946
- Frank & Alice Jolley, 1946-1953
- Robert & Jessie Norcross, Sr., 1953-1967
- Jim Routley (interim), 1967-1968
- Tom & Eileen Richardson, 1968-1978
- George & Ruby Carroll, 1978-1985
- William & Sheila Morrow, 1985-1990
- Bert & Shirley Liira, 1990-1995
- Gary & Pamela Nettleship, 1996-2004
- Tim & Kim Gibb, 2004-current

BETHEL PENTECOSTAL CHURCH:
OTHER PASTORAL STAFF

Over the years, several pastors have assisted in the ministry of Bethel. This list is in alphabetical order by decade.

1940's
Grace Routley (Children's Ministries)

1970's
Paavo Korpela (Youth)

1980's
Ray & Margi Bradbury (Youth)
Paul Carroll (Youth, College & Careers)
Bob & Mildred Clemence (Visitation)
Jerry & Sharon Fulham (Music & Youth)
Grant & Donna Hick (Music & Young Married Couples)
Todd & Ruth Manuel (Youth, College & Careers)
Les & Lois Paulsen (Associate)
Mike & Ann Pierce (Young Married Couples)
Ken & Beverley Powell (Church Ministries)
Charlie & Cora Routley (Visitation)

1990's
Sean & Faith Anderson (Christian Education)
Art & Faith Hambleton (Pastoral Care)
Joel & Mary Heimbecker (Children's Ministries)
Shirley Liira (Music)
Joe & Sarah Manafo (Music, Youth & Junior High)
Steve & Lori Moore (Youth)
Randy & Amanda Raycroft (Youth & Young Adults)
Charlie & Aileen Routley (Visitation to Seniors' Homes)
John & Beverlie Stewart (Youth, College & Careers)
Lyndon & Lori Stratton (Associate & Music)

2000's
Gianpaolo & Alicia Galessiere (Youth, Student Ministries)
Tim & Kim Gibb (Assistant, Associate, Music, Young Adults)
Tricia Gibb (Children's Ministries)
Greg & Melissa Holmes (Assistant)
Joe & Sarah Manafo (Youth & Junior High)
Keith & Patricia Patrick (Associate)
Jamie & Natasha Roberts (Youth)
Domenic Ruso (Assistant Youth, Interim Youth)
Sue Spinks (Children's Ministries)

2010's
Tricia Gibb (Student Ministries)
Keith & Patricia Patrick (Associate)

BETHEL PENTECOSTAL CHURCH: SUPPORT STAFF

Paid staff (both full-time and part-time) have assisted in the ministry of Bethel. These names were sporadically listed in Bethel's Annual Reports, and this list may not be complete.

Office Staff
Wendy Bennett, Bertha Dowswell, Liz Dowswell, Helen Gagnon,
Gail Helps (now Williams), Marilyn Karr, Carol Lee (previously McRae),
Elaine Loten, Karen Overholt, Cherry Schiestel,
Tracy Shannon, Jane Vegh, June Wiebenga

Custodial & Maintenance
George and Janet Antle, Luc & Lynn Labbe, Mike Lunn,
Gerald Mielke, Jack & Linda Kerwin

Student Ministries Assistants
Mary Carruthers, Kim Gibb, Kim Lapier

Communications & Media
Jordan Ouellette, Cayden Gibb

BETHEL PENTECOSTAL CHURCH:
DEACON BOARD MEMBERS (1968-2005) [122]

The Deacon Board was the governing board of the church before 2005, and at various times included up to ten people at one time. In 1999, Grace Celaire became the first woman elected to this board. Continuous records before 1968 were not available.

Roy Allen	Herb Griffith	Russ Pease
Stayley Allen	Chris Guerette	Roy Prendergast
Darwin Armstrong	James Hanley	Wade Priddle
Nelson Brown	Cecil Hannan	Wayne Rabideau
Herb Burdett	Ross Helps	John Rodenhuis
Don Callacott	Dan Helps	Al Roebbelen
Grace Celaire	Mark Holdaway	Charles Routley
Ron Chamberlain	Doug Holmes	Ken Roy
Victor Clark	Greg Hookey	Bill Shaw
Robert Clemence	Ed Huot	John Smith
John Clubb	Carl Johnson	Paul Smith
Roger Collins	Jack Kerwin	George Steensma
Doug Degroot	Harry Knight	Ken Steenwyk
Brad Dilkes	Toan Lai	Dave Strevel
Wilf Doucet	Andy Loscher	Bali Swarath
Orville Douglas	Doug Loten	L. Taylor
Allan Dowswell	Ron Manktelow	Harry Tosh
Bob Dowswell	Almer McCabe	Ken Tosh
Earl Dowswell	Calum McCaskill	Rick VanVeldhuisen
Steve Durocher	Fred Mielke	Bob Vegh
Paul Falconer	John Nanton	Al Walker
Bill Forbes	Dan Nesseth	Dave White
Gary Fournie	Doug Nixon	Ray Worton
Ab Gingrich	Yomi Obiri	
Mahlon Gingrich	Mark Overholt	

BETHEL PENTECOSTAL CHURCH: ELDER BOARD OF DIRECTORS AND DEACON BOARD OF MANAGERS (2006-2016)

In 2005, the church adopted a new constitution, and became an incorporated entity under the Ontario Corporations Act. The new constitution set up two church boards instead of one: an elected Elder Board of Directors, which serves as the governing board, and an appointed Deacon Board of Managers, which serves under the authority of the Elder Board. Constitutionally, the Elder Board is to serve the church and assist the Pastor in matters pertaining to the assembly and its spiritual life and mission, whereas the Deacon Board is to assist in the management of the church's financial, business, and property matters. The first Elder Board of Directors was elected in March 2006. An asterisk (*) denotes an honorary title only, not a constitutional office.

Elder Board of Directors (2006-2016)

Darwin Armstrong	Chris Guerette	Derek Shannon
Grace Celaire	Doug Holmes	John Skinner
Caleb Courtney	Harry & Ann Knight*	Ken Steenwyk
Louis Debrum	Doug Nixon	Dave Strevel
Bob Foster	Yomi Obiri	Jack Tunstill
Steve Fraser	Wade Priddle	Ray & Rita Worton*

Deacon Board of Managers (2006-2016)

James Bird	Ken Lapier	Joe Sit
Steve Fraser	Scott Maidman	Shannon Smith
Bob Foster	Dave Ouellette	Dave Strevel
Brian Gagnon	Matt Routley	Duncan Tunstill
George Irving	Derek Shannon	Hank Visser*

AVERAGE SUNDAY ATTENDANCE

These statistics are from Bethel's annual reports. Average attendance statistics from before 1979 were not readily available.

Year	S.S.	AM	PM	Year	S.S.	AM	PM
1979	197	199	139	1999	174	496	271
1980	248	271	186	2000	148	430	274
1981	286	347	234	2001	167	432	267
1982	323	503	345	2002	155	458	249
1983	357	549	390	2003	124	435	226
1984	361	616	376	2004	78	410	195
1985	339	607	403	2005	N/A	404	166
1986	312	615	366	2006	N/A	400	219
1987	306	604	346	2007	N/A	385	175
1988	348	610	366	2008	N/A	338	135
1989	314	630	375	2009	N/A	336	115
1990	291	631	387	2010	N/A	343	112
1991	295	615	384	2011	N/A	375	121
1992	264	589	384	2012	N/A	379	129
1993	238	570	367	2013	N/A	415	181
1994	217	599	348	2014	N/A	435	122
1995	179	545	297	2015	N/A	399	115
1996	250	609	343				
1997	220	626	401				
1998	195	589	377				

*S.S. = Sunday School.

Photo Credits

Zelma Argue: 14; from her book, *A Vision and a Vow, or, The Vision and Vow of a Canadian Maiden: The Story of My Mother's Life* (Springfield: Gospel Publishing House, 1945).

Bethel Pentecostal Church: cover, 19, 23, 27, 28, 32, 37, 38, 39, 41, 44, 45, 46, 48, 52, 54, 55, 56, 62.

Caleb Courtney: 17, 38.

The Canadian Baptist Archives: 7; from "Barbara Johnstone," *The McMaster University Monthly XVI: October 1906 to May 1907* (Toronto: The Miln-Bingham Printing Company, 1907), 372.

Dorothy Dunne: 24, 34.

Allen Froese: 53; from his website, www.allenfroese.com.

Tim Gibb: 49, 58.

Dan & Patti Helps: 47.

Master's Pentecostal Seminary: 3.

Martin McCabe: 25.

Alawode Oluwasegun: 62.

Parry Sound Pentecostal Tabernacle: 12; from *Parry Sound Pentecostal Tabernacle: Sixty Years of Service* (Parry Sound: Parry Sound Printing, 1972).

The Pentecostal Assemblies of Canada Archives: 22, 26, 29, 31, 42; from various sources, including *The Pentecostal Testimony*.

The Queen's Printer for Ontario: xii; from the *Ontario Official Government Road Map: 1937-1938* (Toronto: The Government of Ontario Travel and Publicity Bureau, 1937).

Perry Routley: 28.

The Sarnia Canadian Observer: 15, 16, 35.

Shake The Nations: 59.

Unknown (1930's postcards): ix, 20.

The Western Ontario District of the Pentecostal Assemblies of Canada: 23, 24.

Notes

[1] Some Pentecostal writers have claimed that the Azusa Street Revival was the source of the global Pentecostal revival at the turn of the twentieth century, but scholars are increasingly appealing to evidence that there were many independent Pentecostal revivals happening simultaneously around the world. For one scholar's take on this, see Adam Stewart, "From Monogenesis to Polygenesis in Pentecostal Origins: A Survey of the Evidence from the Azusa Street, Hebden and Mukti Missions," *PentecoStudies: An Interdisciplinary Journal for Research on the Pentecostal and Charismatic Movements* 13.2 (2014): 151-172.

[2] "How Holy Roller Gets Religion," Los Angeles Herald, 10 September 1906, 7.

[3] Ellen Hebden, "In Toronto, Canada," *The Apostolic Faith* 1.7, April 1907, 1; Ellen Hebden, "This is the Power of the Holy Ghost," *The Apostolic Faith* 1.6, February-March 1907, 4; "Number Received Baptism," *The Apostolic Faith* 1.5, January 1907, 1; A. S. Copley, "Pentecost in Toronto," *The Apostolic Faith* 1.5, January 1907, 4; "Report of O. Adams," *The Apostolic Faith* 1.4, December 1906, 3.

[4] J. Loney, "Snowflake, Manitoba," *The Apostolic Faith* 1.4, December 1906, 3.

[5] "Pentecost in Winnipeg, Manitoba," *The Apostolic Faith* 1.9, June 1907, 1; "Testimonies: T. Anderson," *The Apostolic Faith* 1.12, January 1908, 4; "Testimonies: K. Scott," *The Apostolic Faith* 1.12, January 1908, 4; "Winnipeg, Can.," *The Apostolic Faith* 1.12, January 1908, 1.

[6] For an excellent treatment of the history of James and Ellen Hebden, see William Sloos, "The Story of James and Ellen Hebden: The First Family of Pentecost in Canada," *Pneuma* 32.2 (2010): 181-202. For another history of Canadian Pentecostal origins, in two parts, see Thomas William Miller, "The Canadian Jerusalem: The Story of James and Ellen Hebden and Their Toronto

Mission (Part 1)," *Assemblies of God Heritage* 11.3 (1991): 5-7, 22-23, <http://ifphc.org/pdf/Heritage/1991_03.pdf>; Thomas William Miller, "The Canadian Jerusalem: The Story of James and Ellen Hebden and Their Toronto Mission (Part 2)," *Assemblies of God Heritage* 11.4 (1991): 22-31, <http://ifphc.org/pdf/Heritage/1991_04.pdf>.

[7] Ellen Hebden, "How Pentecost Came To Toronto," *The Promise* 1, May 1907: 1-3.

[8] James Hebden, "In sending the first number of The Promise," *The Promise* 1, May 1907, 1.

[9] *Ibid.*

[10] "Praise and Prayer," *Mukti Prayer-Bell* 4.3, November 1909, 1. This newsletter clarifies that "Miss Barbara Johnstone of Sarnia, Ontario, Canada, is now Mrs. John Norton."

[11] Lawrence A. Crich, *The Way It Was: The History of the Sarnia Public Elementary Schools* (Sarnia: s.p., 1986), 65.

[12] Mrs. John Norton, "Testimony" *Jehovah-Jireh: A Witness to Christ's Faithfulness* 1.4, December 1909.

[13] At the time of Barbara Johnton's graduation in 1907, McMaster University was located in Toronto, Ontario, at the current site of the Royal Conservatory of Music on Bloor Street West, just west of Avenue Road. This was just five kilometres from the Hebden's East End Mission at 651 Queen Street East. McMaster University moved to its current location in Hamilton, Ontario, in 1929.

[14] Ibid.

[15] *1908 Sarnia City Directory.*

[16] Norton, "Testimony."

[17] *Jehovah-Jireh: A Witness to Christ's Faithfulness* 1.2, January 1909, 9.

[18] "Face to Face," *Mukti Prayer-Bell* 5.2, January 1912, 3-4.

[19] "Barbara Johnstone," *The McMaster University Monthly XVI: October 1906 to May 1907* (Toronto: The Miln-Bingham Printing Company, 1907), 372.

[20] Norton, "Testimony."

[21] Charles Parham was the first in the Pentecostal movement to associate *glossolalia*—the technical term for "speaking in tongues"—with the baptism of the Holy Spirit.

[22] Agnes Ozman, "Where the Latter Rain First Fell: The First One to Speak in Tongues," *Latter Rain Evangel* 1.4, January 1909, 2.

[23] See Sarah E. Parham, *The Life of Charles F. Parham* (Baxter Springs: s.p., 1930), 52.

[24] Classical Pentecostal denominations that ascribe to the doctrine of initial evidence include, among others, the Assemblies of God (Springfield, Missouri), the Pentecostal Assemblies of Canada (Mississauga, Ontario), the Church of God (Cleveland, Tennessee), the Church of God in Christ (Memphis, Tennessee), the International Pentecostal Holiness Church (Oklahoma City, Oklahoma), and the International Church of the Foursquare Gospel (Los Angeles, California). For further academic study on this point, see Roger Stronstad, *The Charismatic Theology of St. Luke* (Grand Rapids: Baker Academic, 2012). For an excellent book about the Holy Spirit see Anthony D. Palma, *The Holy Spirit: A Pentecostal Perspective* (Springfield: Gospel Publishing House, 2001).

[25] *1928 Sarnia City Directory.*

[26] A few decades later, on October 28, 1944, a Christian Book Store would also emerge on Victoria Street. This subsequent book store was operated by some of the congregation of Temple Baptist Church in Sarnia. See W. H. MacBain, *A Tree Planted by the River: The Story of Temple Baptist Church, Sarnia, Ontario, 1937-1987* (Sarnia: Temple Baptist Church, 1986), 25-26.

[27] Cecil M. Robeck, *Azusa Street Mission & Revival: The Birth of the Global Pentecostal Movement* (Nashville: Thomas Nelson, Inc., 2006), 327.

[28] See Steven Jack Land, *Pentecostal Spirituality: A Passion for the Kingdom* (Cleveland: CPT Press, 2010).

[29] "Brief Mention," *The Pentecostal Testimony* 10.5, May 1929, 19.

[30] "Items of Interest," *The Pentecostal Testimony* 10.6, June 1929, 21.

[31] Frank Reginald Jolley, PAOC Application for Affiliation, 1931.

[32] The 1921 Canada Census lists the entire family as "Pentecostal." This included a 17-year-old Frank, along with his dad, Ambrose Charles Jolley, his mom, Lucie, and his siblings—an older brother, Jack, and a younger sister, Agnes. The Jolley family had immigrated from England in 1910. See Library and Archives Canada, *Sixth Census of Canada, 1921* (Ottawa: Library and Archives Canada, 2013)

[33] "Wedding Bells," *The Pentecostal Testimony* 10.7, July 1929, 6.

[34] "Go to Church Sunday! Pentecostal Assembly," *The Sarnia Canadian Observer*, Sarnia, Ontario, Saturday, May 25, 1929, 11.

[35] "Wedding Bells," *The Pentecostal Testimony* 12.2, February 1931, 2.

[36] Gordon Atter's father, Arthur Atter, had been a part of the Hebden's "East End Mission" at 651 Queen Street in Toronto. Gordon Atter, at this time a pastor, would later become a prominent teacher at Eastern Pentecostal Bible College in Peterborough, Ontario, and authored several Pentecostal leaflets, books, and Bible College materials along the way.

[37] "Opening of the New Tabernacle in Strathroy, Ont.," *The Pentecostal Testimony* 14.12, December 1933, 11.

[38] "Showers of Blessing in Sarnia, Ont.," *The Pentecostal Testimony* 16.2, February 1935, 12.

[39] Valone Sly, Eunice Morris, and Viola Haskim, *Parry Sound Pentecostal Tabernacle: Sixty Years of Service* (Parry Sound: Parry Sound Printing, 1972), 21. Stephan was an interim pastor in Parry Sound shortly after George Chambers, who would become the General Superintendent of the PAOC.

[40] James F. Kelley, "Healed of Stammering and Stuttering," *The Canadian Pentecostal Testimony* 4.1, January 1925, 2.

[41] "Showers of Blessing," 12.

[42] *1935 Sarnia City Directory.*

[43] *1934 Sarnia City Directory.*

[44] Pastor and evangelist Rev. George Tunks (1918-2008), known for his preaching, which was full of conviction, and his quirky sense of humour, was saved and filled with the Spirit at the "Bothwell Revival" in 1938, when he was twenty years old. See V. G. Brown, ed., *Fifty Years of Pentecostal History: 1933-1983* (Burlington, Ontario: The Pentecostal Assemblies of Canada, 1983), 31-32. See also George Tunks and David Kitz, *Tunks on Tongues* (Winnipeg, Manitoba: Forever Books, 2010), 24-25, 104.

[45] "Sarnia, Ont.," *The Pentecostal Testimony* 16.6, June 1935, 14.

[46] The Argue Evangelistic Party was comprised of the family of Andrew Harvey Argue of Winnipeg, Manitoba. He, along with several of his children including two of his daughters, Beulah and Zelma, and two of his sons, Watson and Elwin, were itinerant evangelists, and referred to themselves collectively as "The Argue Evangelistic Party" in their own newsletter. See *The Revival Broadcast* 1.1, December 1923, 1.

[47] "How Stars Are Made Evangelist's Topic," *The Sarnia Canadian Observer*, Sarnia, Ontario, Wednesday, January 2, 1935, 3.

[48] "Angler Fell Through Ice In Sarnia Bay: Evangelist Argue To Rescue," *The Sarnia Canadian Observer*, Sarnia, Ontario, Monday, March 14, 1938, 3.

[49] "Sarnia, Ont.," *The Pentecostal Testimony* 19.4, April 1938, 9.

50 "Tomorrow at Church: Full Gospel Tabernacle," *The Sarnia Canadian Observer*, Sarnia, Ontario, Saturday, February 26, 1938, 5.

51 "Tomorrow at Church: Gospel Tabernacle," *The Sarnia Canadian Observer*, Sarnia, Ontario, Saturday, March 12, 1938, 5; "Tomorrow at Church: Gospel Tabernacle," *The Sarnia Canadian Observer*, Sarnia, Ontario, Saturday, March 19, 1938, 5.

52 Russ Pease, ed., *Bethel Church, Sarnia, Ontario: 50th Anniversary, 1936-1986* (Sarnia: Haines Printing, 1986), 7.

53 "Pastor and Mrs. S. H. Wilson and the Great Chatham and Bothwell Crusade for Christ," *The Pentecostal Testimony* 17.11, December 1936, 10. The Wilsons planted numerous churches in the area. For example, see Peter Epp, *The History of Evangel Pentecostal Tabernacle, Dresden, Ontario: 1939-2014* (Dresden: s.p., 2014).

54 Rev. Max Powers lived from 1907 to 1947, and had served as a missionary to Igbeti, Nigeria, from 1929-1932. See James Clare Fuller, *We Trust God Will Own His Word: A Holiness-Mennonite Mission in Nigeria 1905-1978*, ThM Thesis, McMaster University, Hamilton, Ontario, 2003, 59. More insight about Rev. Powers comes from the "Obituary of Ruth Anna Fick (formerly Powers, née Wooll)," *The London Free Press*, London, Ontario, January 18, 2006: "[Ruth Anna Wooll] met a young Canadian Evangelist, the Reverend George Max Powers, senior. They fell in love, were married, moved to Sarnia, had four daughters and later moved to Walsingham [near Tillsonburg, Ontario] where George pastored the Free Methodist church; there they had a son. George died of cancer in 1947 and Ruth continued as a lay pastor in Walsingham for the next three years."

55 George Carroll, ed., *Bethel Church: Sarnia, Ontario* (Sarnia: s.p., 1980), 2.

56 The history of the Apostolic Church in Great Britain simply states, "An outpost was established at Sarnia (Ontario) and led by W. J. McKeown." See James E. Worsfold, *The Origins of the Apostolic Church in Great Britain* (Wellington, New Zealand: Julian Literature Trust, 1991), 225.

57 The Apostolic Church in Canada is not to be confused with the denomination of a similar name, the Apostolic Church of Pentecost of Canada.

58 C. E. L. Walls, "Allan—Rev. David," *The Canadian Free Methodist Herald* 18.2, 1 October 1940, 7.

59 E. E. Loveless, "Gibson—Margaret Jane Pollock," death notice from a newspaper clipping, about January 1929.

[60] William Alexander Gibson (1857-1925) and Margaret Jane Pollock (1857-1929) had eight children altogether: Maude Mary Jane (1879-1967), Elizabeth Ella (b. 1882), Pearl Charlotte (1884-1961), Victoria May (b. 1886), Margaret Ann (b. 1888), Edna A. (1890-1967), Sarah Grace (b. 1892), and William Ernest (1894-1915).

[61] "Ohio Marriages, 1800-1958," FamilySearch database, John Riblet and Edna Durrance, 31 Dec 1908, Lucas, Ohio, FHL microfilm 2,131,984, <https://familysearch.org/pal:/MM9.1.1/XDXG-JBP>.

[62] Edna Riblet is listed as a dressmaker in various years of the *Sarnia City Directory*, living at 226 Durand Street (1924), 374 N. Russell Street (1925), 379 Maxwell Street (1930), and then again at 374 N. Russell Street (1937). This was also reported on the 1921 Census of Canada.

[63] Pease, *Bethel Church, Sarnia, Ontario: 50th Anniversary*, 6. Also, "Sunday School in What is Known as Shanty Town—Sarnia," *The Pentecostal Testimony* 20.5, May 1939, 11.

[64] Jack West and Harold Davis, *They Call Him Mr. Braeside: The Life Story of J. H. Blair* (Toronto: Harmony Printing, n.d.), 54-55.

[65] *Ibid.*, 59.

[66] From July 1-17, 1938, Braeside Camp hosted evangelist A. A. Wilson of Kansas City, Missouri, principal W. I. Evans of Springfield, Missouri, and the Henry family from Tulsa, Oklahoma. See "Camp Meeting Time: Braeside Camp," *The Pentecostal Testimony* 19.5, May 1938, 12-13.

[67] For a recent take on this theme see The Pentecostal Assemblies of Canada, *Authentically Pentecostal*, ed. David Wells and Van Johnson (Mississauga: The Pentecostal Assemblies of Canada International Office, 2010).

[68] See Donald Dayton, *Theological Roots of Pentecostalism* (Peabody: Hendrickson Publishers, 1987), 21.

[69] Greg Holmes, "The History of Bethel Pentecostal Church," *If He Builds It They Will Come* (Shippensburg: Destiny Image Publishers, Inc., 2007), 71.

[70] "Shanty Town—Sarnia," 11.

[71] Pease, *Bethel Church, Sarnia, Ontario: 50th Anniversary*, 7.

[72] James Lewis Hammond was born on May 24, 1882 in Jordan, Ontario, and died on March 25, 1948 in Dunnville, Ontario. His first wife, Mary Jane Lambier, died on August 12, 1938 in Dunnville, Ontario. See Nelson Denton, "Re: McIntee families Louth Twp.," 26 August 2003, 15 September 2016, <http://archiver.rootsweb.ancestry.com/th/read/NIAGARA-ONT/2003-08/1061916831>.

[73] "Sarnia, Ontario," *The Pentecostal Testimony* 22.12, 1 December 1941, 16.

[74] Almond Obadiah Routley was born on March 2, 1886 in Victoria County, Ontario, and died on August 4, 1961 at Shepherd's Lodge in Agincourt, Ontario. He married Lydia Victoria McAmmond (1887-1969) in Saskatoon, Saskatchewan on December 21, 1909. Both A. O. and Lydia Routley are buried at the Cobourg Union Cemetery in Cobourg, Ontario. See Claudia and Terry Boorman, "Kerfoot Genealogy Report" 26 December 2014, 11 October 2016, <http://boormanfamily.ca/trees/kerfoot/rr01/rr01_039.htm>.

[75] Almond Obadiah Routley, Clergy Record, PAOC Archives.

[76] Sarnia's Polymer factory was so successful that it would be commemoratively featured on Canada's 1971 ten-dollar bill.

[77] A young Almer McCabe gave the first $50.00 to the building fund. See Carroll, *Bethel Church*, 3.

[78] Some of A. O. Routley's grandchildren, great-grandchildren, and great-great-grandchildren attend Bethel Pentecostal Church today, and continue to be ministry leaders and active members in the life of the church.

[79] "New Church Dedicated at Sarnia, Ontario," *The Pentecostal Testimony* 30.3, 15 March 1949, 15.

[80] Joyce Gingrich, née Thompson, lived from May 28, 1934 to September 24, 2010. She played the piano at the Essex Street church and later at the London Line church, until her hands became painfully weak with arthritis. Even then, she would occasionally do a special Christmas number, or an offertory, with Dorothy Dunne, the church organist.

[81] Adeline Elizabeth Stephan, Clergy Record, PAOC Archives.

[82] "New Church Dedicated at Sarnia, Ontario," 15.

[83] *Ibid.*

[84] "Sarnia, Ontario," *The Pentecostal Testimony* 30.8, 15 August 1949, 16. For a similar description of C. S. Tubby, as well as his photo, see "Services Will Be Conducted in Large Tent: Shamokin Gospel Tabernacle Will Hold Tent Meetings at Ferndale," *Shamokin News-Dispatch*, Shamokin, Pennsylvania, Saturday, June 17, 1939, 3.

[85] The late George Chambers, former General Superintendent of the PAOC remembered a 1912 camp meeting in Vineland, Ontario, writing, "For example, one morning at about 2:00 a.m. there were those who were still praying and seeking God for the baptism of the Holy Spirit." George Chambers, *50 Years of Service of the King: 1907-1957* (Toronto: The Testimony Press, 1960), 20.

[86] "Sarnia, Ontario" (1949), 16.

[87] Mrs. Edna Riblet (Mrs. J. L. Hammond), Clergy Record, PAOC Archives.

[88] Sly, et al., *Parry Sound Pentecostal Tabernacle*, 33.

[89] Bertha Dowswell, "1936-1996," in *Great Is Thy Faithfulness: Bethel Pentecostal Church, 60th Anniversary, 1936-1996*, ed. Joyce Gingrich (Sarnia: Bethel Pentecostal Church, 1996), 8-9.

[90] *Ibid.*

[91] A. O. Routley lived from March 2, 1886 to August 4, 1961, and had nine children with his wife Lydia—four boys and five girls—many of whom became pastors: Frank, Charlie, David, Jim, Grace, Margaret, Violet, Barbara, and Gertrude.

[92] Harry Tosh was also responsible for building and installing Braeside Camp's water distribution system, including pumps, tanks, and filtration system, which is still in use today. Harry Tosh's son, Ken, would become a longtime member of Bethel, serving on the board for many years, and volunteering to participate and assist the new church in Bright's Grove for ten years.

[93] "Pentecostal: Bethel Pentecostal Church," *The Sarnia Observer*, Sarnia, Ontario, Saturday, November 5, 2016, 3.

[94] Paul Morden, "Long-Time Organist Marks 60 Years," *The Sarnia Observer*, Sarnia, Ontario, Friday, February 5, 2016, A1-A2.

[95] Dorothy Dunne, "I Won't Easily Forget," in *Great Is Thy Faithfulness: Bethel Pentecostal Church, 60th Anniversary, 1936-1996*, ed. Joyce Gingrich (Sarnia: Bethel Pentecostal Church, 1996), 9.

[96] Goodreads, Inc., "Donna (Sarnia, ON, Canada)'s Review," 16 April 2014, 15 September 2016, <http://www.goodreads.com/review/show/852230159>.

[97] A few years later, Ab Gingrich would be the Project Manager for the new Temple Baptist Church at 1410 Quinn Drive in Sarnia, Ontario. See MacBain, *Temple Baptist Church*, 121.

[98] Carroll, *Bethel Church*, 4.

[99] "Sod Turned at New Church Site," *The Sarnia Observer*, 1979.

[100] Rev. William D. Morrow became a part of the faculty at EPBC beginning in 1980. See Emma E. Hann, *Reflections of Eastern Pentecostal Bible College* (Peterborough: Eastern Pentecostal Bible College Alumni Association, 1986), 36.

[101] William D. Morrow, *Potential for Ministry*, DMin Thesis, United Theological Seminary, Dayton, Ohio, December 1996, 17.

[102] See Brown, *Fifty Years of Pentecostal History*, 41. See also Jean Turnbull Elford, *Canada West's Last Frontier: A History of Lambton* (Sarnia, Ontario: Lambton County Historical Society, 1983), 67. Note that Elford incorrectly

indicates that Courtright Pentecostal Church was established in 1963 (the correct year is 1957).

[103] David Rutledge, *Telephone Interview* Caleb Courtney, 9 November 2016.

[104] Shirley Liira, "Ministry of Music Report," *1990 Annual Report* (Sarnia: Bethel Pentecostal Church, 1991), 2.

[105] Bert Liira, *Telephone Interview* Caleb Courtney, 28 October 2016.

[106] Charlie Routley, "Minister of Visitation to Seniors' Homes," *1998 Annual Report* (Sarnia: Bethel Pentecostal Church, 1999), 11.

[107] I am indebted to Ken and Val Tosh for sharing their memories of this era.

[108] The topic of revival is a fascinating one. "Revival" has typically been understood as a temporary, sovereign move of God that brings extraordinary blessing and empowerment for witness. "Renewal," on the other hand, is when God's people are convicted of sin, pursue his purposes, and seek his power anew in their lives.

[109] Margaret Gibb spoke at the Congress on Pentecostal Leadership (COPL '87) on October 20, 1987, on the topic of "A Woman's Place of Ministry in a Pentecostal Church."

[110] Women have always played an integral part in Pentecostal evangelism. Within the PAOC, women had been granted a "Deaconess" or "Ministerial License for Women" credential, but had not been formally "ordained," although in common practice, the "Ministerial License for Women" was roughly equivalent to this. In 1984, women were officially granted the right to be ordained ministers in the PAOC, and in 1998, they were granted to right to hold executive positions at the national level of leadership. See Pamela M. S. Holmes, "Ministering Women in the Pentecostal Assemblies of Canada," *Canadian Pentecostalism: Transition and Transformation*, ed. Michael Wilkinson (Montreal: McGill-Queen's University Press, 2009): 171-194. For Sarnia's local news coverage about the 1984 decision, see "Ordination of Women Granted Approval by Pentecostal Assemblies of Canada," *The Sarnia Observer*, Tuesday, October 9, 1984.

[111] Holmes, "The History of Bethel Pentecostal Church," 86.

[112] Tim Gibb, *The 06 Sarnia Revival* (Sarnia: Bethel Pentecostal Church, 2016), 4. This meeting occurred at Bethel on October 30, 2005.

[113] *Ibid.*, 2.

[114] Cathy Dobson, "'Faith Healer' Sent Home," *The Sarnia Observer*, Friday, June 2, 2006, 1; Cathy Dobson, "'Faith Healer' Back in Class," *The Sarnia Observer*, Saturday, June 3, 2006, 1.

---

[115] I am indebted to the back issues of Bethel's monthly *CONNECT* bulletins for information from 2011-2016. Bethel Sarnia, *Bethel Sarnia - issuu*, September 2016, 14 September 2016, <https://issuu.com/bethelsarnia/docs>.

[116] Tim Gibb, "Atmospheres, Climates, and Cultures," *CONNECT* February 2011.

[117] Charles McAmmond Routley, who lived from July 17, 1919 to April 14, 2016 held credentials with the PAOC and upon his passing was honoured along with several others at the PAOC General Conference in Montreal in May 2016.

[118] Robeck, *Azusa Street Mission & Revival*, 327.

[119] West and Davis, "Mr. Braeside," 49.

[120] Raymond L. Cox, *The Four-Square Gospel* (Los Angeles: Foursquare Publications, 1969), 9.

[121] Dayton, *Theological Roots of Pentecostalism*, 21-22.

[122] This list updates a pre-existing list of Board Members from 1968-1996 that was compiled for Bethel's 60th anniversary. See Joyce Gingrich, ed., *Great Is Thy Faithfulness: Bethel Pentecostal Church, 60th Anniversary, 1936-1996* (Sarnia: Bethel Pentecostal Church, 1996), 10.

Selected Bibliography

EARLY 20TH CENTURY NEWSLETTERS

The Apostolic Faith. Los Angeles, California. 1906-1908.

The Apostolic Messenger. Winnipeg, Manitoba. 1908.

The Good Report. Ottawa, Ontario. 1910-1913.

Jehovah-Jireh: A Witness to Christ's Faithfulness. Poona, India. 1909-1913.

The Pentecostal Testimony. Toronto, Ontario. 1920-present.

The Promise. Toronto, Ontario. 1906-1910.

The Revival Broadcast. Winnipeg, Manitoba. 1923-1928.

LOCAL SARNIA HISTORY

Burwell, Dave, et al. *Sarnia: 100 Years, 1914-2014*. Sarnia, Ontario: The Community Round Table, 2014.

Carroll, George A., ed. *Bethel Church, Sarnia, Ontario*. Sarnia, Ontario: Bethel Pentecostal Church, 1980.

Crich, Lawrence A. *The Way It Was: The History of the Sarnia Public Elementary Schools.* Sarnia, Ontario: s.p., 1986.

Elford, Jean Turnbull. *Canada West's Last Frontier: A History of Lambton.* Sarnia, Ontario: Lambton County Historical Society, 1983.

Gibb, Tim. *Sarnia Revival 06.* Sarnia, Ontario: Bethel Pentecostal Church, 2016,

—. *Building Our Future.* Sarnia, Ontario: Bethel Pentecostal Church, 2016.

Holmes, Greg. *If He Builds It They Will Come.* Shippensburg, Pennsylvania: Destiny Image Publishers, Inc., 2007.

MacBain, W. H. *A Tree Planted by the River: The Story of Temple Baptist Church, Sarnia, Ontario, 1937-1987.* Sarnia, Ontario: Temple Baptist Church, 1986.

Pease, Russ, ed. *Bethel Church, Sarnia, Ontario: 50th Anniversary, 1936-1986.* Sarnia, Ontario: Bethel Pentecostal Church, 1986.

Phelps, Edward. *A Bibliography of Lambton County and the City of Sarnia, Ontario.* London, Ontario: General Library, University of Western Ontario, 1970. Library Bulletin Series, No. 8.

The Sarnia Canadian Observer. Sarnia, Ontario. 1853-present.

PENTECOSTALISM IN CANADA

Argue, Zelma. *A Vision and A Vow, or, The Vision and Vow of a Canadian Maiden: The Story of My Mother's Life.* Springfield, Missouri: Gospel Publishing House, 1945.

Atter, Gordon Francis. *The Pentecostal Movement: Who We Are and What We Believe.* Humberstone, Ontario: s.p., 1937.

—. *The Third Force*. 3rd. Peterborough, Ontario: The College Press, 1970.

Brown, Victor G., ed. *Fifty Years of Pentecostal History: 1933-1983*. Burlington, Ontario: The Pentecostal Assemblies of Canada, 1983.

Canadian Journal of Pentecostal-Charismatic Christianity. Trinity Western University. Langley, British Columbia, 2010-present. <https://journal.twu.ca/index.php/CJPC/issue/archive>.

Chambers, George A. *Fifty Years in the Service of the King: 1907-1957*. Toronto, Ontario: The Testimony Press, 1960.

Collier, Michael J. *Pentecostal Nova Scotia: Sketches in History*. Unpublished Paper. Mount Saint Vincent University. Halifax, Nova Scotia, 1980.

Connect. Bethel Pentecostal Church. Sarnia, Ontario, 2011-present. <https://issuu.com/bethelsarnia/docs>.

Di Giacomo, Michael. *Les Assemblées de la Pentecôte: leur origine, leur évolution, leur théologie distinctive*. MA Thesis. Université Laval. Laval, Quebec, 1994.

Drewitz, Arthur. *A History of the German Branch of the Pentecostal Assemblies of Canada*. Kitchener, Ontario: German Branch of the Pentecostal Assemblies of Canada, 1986.

The Evangelical Fellowship of Canada. Thesis Papers and Dissertations on Canadian Evangelicalism. 2016. <http://www.evangelicalfellowship.ca/page.aspx?pid=4112>.

Fortune, C. Roy. *Tongues in the Valley: A History of Twentieth Century Ottawa Valley Pentecostalism*. Kanata, Ontario: s.p., 2008.

Hawkes, Paul Stewart. *Pentecostalism in Canada: A History with Implications for the Future*. DMin Thesis. San Francisco Theological Seminary. San Anselmo, California, 1982.

—. *Songs of the Reaper: The Story of the Pentecostal Assemblies of Canada in Saskatchewan*. Saskatoon, Saskatchewan: The Pentecostal Assemblies of Canada Saskatchewan District, 1985.

Jaenen, Cornelius J. *The Pentecostal Movement*. MA Thesis. University of Manitoba. Winnipeg, Manitoba, 1950.

Janes, Burton K. *History of the Pentecostal Assemblies of Newfoundland*. St. John's, Newfoundland: The Pentecostal Assemblies of Newfoundland, 1996.

Klan, Donald. *Pentecostal Assemblies of Canada Church Growth in British Columbia from Origins until 1953*. MCS Thesis. Regent College. Vancouver, British Columbia, 1979.

Kulbeck, Gloria Grace. *What God Hath Wrought: A History of the Pentecostal Assemblies of Canada*. Toronto, Ontario: The Pentecostal Assemblies of Canada, 1958.

Kydd, Ronald A. N. "The Pentecostal Assemblies of Canada and Society." *The Canadian Society of Church History Papers (1972-1973)*. Queen's University. Kingston, Ontario, 1973: 1-15.

Larden, Robert A. *Our Apostolic Heritage: An Official History of the Apostolic Church of Pentecost of Canada Incorporated*. Calgary, Alberta: Apostolic Church of Pentecost of Canada Incorporated, 1971.

MacKay, Garth. *The Emergence of Religious Organizations in Western Prince Edward Island, 1900-1950*. Unpublished Paper. University of Prince Edward Island. Charlottetown, Prince Edward Island, 1984.

Miller, Thomas William. *Canadian Pentecostals: A History of the Pentecostal Assemblies of Canada*. Mississauga, Ontario: Full Gospel Publishing House, 1994.

—. "The Canadian Jerusalem: The Story of James and Ellen Hebden and Their Toronto Mission (Part 1)." *Assemblies of God Heritage* 11.3 (1991): 5-7, 22-23. <http://ifphc.org/pdf/Heritage/1991_03.pdf>.

—. "The Canadian Jerusalem: The Story of James and Ellen Hebden and Their Toronto Mission (Part 2)." *Assemblies of God Heritage* 11.4 (1991): 22-31. <http://ifphc.org/pdf/Heritage/1991_04.pdf>.

—. "The Significance of A.H. Argue for Pentecostal Historiography." *Pneuma* 8.1 (1986): 120-158.

Morsch, J. Shirley, et al., eds. *Rejoice: A History of the Pentecostal Assemblies of Alberta and the Northwest Territories*. Edmonton, Alberta: The Pentecostal Assemblies of Canada Alberta and Northwest Territories (MacKenzie) District, 1983.

The Pentecostal Assemblies of Canada. *The Pentecostal Assemblies of Canada: A Brief History*. Toronto, Ontario: Full Gospel Publishing House, 1976.

—. *Canadian Pentecostal History Bibliography*. 2016. <https://paoc.org/docs/default-source/paoc-family-docs/Archives/Academic-Resources/canadian-pentecostal-history-bibliography.pdf>.

Purdie, J. Eustace. *Concerning The Faith*. Toronto, Ontario: The Full Gospel Publishing House, 1951.

Rudd, Douglas. *When The Spirit Came Upon Them: Highlights from the Early Years of the Pentecostal Movement in Canada*. Burlington, Ontario: Antioch Books, 2002.

Slauenwhite, David C. *An Historical Perspective on the Pentecostal Assemblies of Canada: 75th Anniversary Report.* Calgary, Alberta: The Pentecostal Assemblies of Canada, 1994.

Sloos, William. "The Story of James and Ellen Hebden: The First Family of Pentecost in Canada." *Pneuma* 32.2 (2010): 181-202.

Sly, Valone, et al. *Parry Sound Pentecostal Tabernacle: Sixty Years of Service.* Parry Sound, Ontario: s.p., 1972

Stiller, Brian Carl. *The Evolution of Pentecostalism: From Sectarianism to Denominationalism: With Special Reference to The Danforth Gospel Temple 1922-1968.* MRel Thesis. Wycliffe College. Toronto, Ontario, 1975.

Tunks, George, and David Kitz. *Tunks on Tongues.* Winnipeg, Manitoba: Forever Books, 2010.

Wegner, Linda. *Streams of Grace: A History of the Apostolic Church of Pentecost of Canada.* Edmonton, Alberta: New Leaf Works, 2006.

Wells, David and Van Johnson, ed. *Authentically Pentecostal.* Mississauga, Ontario: The Pentecostal Assemblies of Canada International Office, 2010.

West, Jack, and Harold Davis. *They Call Him Mr. Braeside: The Life Story of Rev. J. H. Blair.* Toronto, Ontario: s.p., 1970.

Whitt, Irving Alfred. *Developing a Pentecostal Missiology in the Canadian Context (1867-1944): The Pentecostal Assemblies of Canada.* DMiss Thesis. Fuller Theological Seminary. Pasadena, California, 1994.

Wilkinson, Michael, ed. *Canadian Pentecostalism: Transition and Transformation.* Montreal, Quebec: McGill-Queen's University Press, 2009.

—. *The Spirit Said Go: Pentecostal Immigrants in Canada*. New York, New York: Peter Lang Publishing, Inc., 2006.

Wilkinson, Michael and Peter Althouse. *Winds from the North: Canadian Contributions to the Pentecostal Movement*. Leiden, Netherlands: Brill, 2010.

GENERAL PENTECOSTAL WORKS

Anderson, Allan. *An Introduction to Pentecostalism*. New York, New York: Cambridge University Press, 2004.

Dayton, Donald W. *Theological Roots of Pentecostalism*. Peabody, Massachusetts: Hendrickson Publishers, 1987.

Kay, William K. *Pentecostalism: A Very Short Introduction*. New York, New York: Oxford University Press, 2011.

Palma, Anthony D. *The Holy Spirit: A Pentecostal Perspective*. Springfield, Missouri: Gospel Publishing House, 2001.

Robeck, Cecil M., Jr. *The Azusa Street Mission & Revival: The Birth of the Global Pentecostal Movement*. Nashville, Tennessee: Thomas Nelson, Inc., 2006.

Robeck, Cecil M., Jr. and Amos Yong, *The Cambridge Companion to Pentecostalism*. New York, New York: Cambridge University Press, 2014.

Stronstad, Roger. *The Charismatic Theology of St. Luke: Trajectories from the Old Testament to Luke-Acts*. Grand Rapids, Michigan: Baker Academic, 2012.

Wacker, Grant. *Heaven Below: Early Pentecostals and American Culture*. Cambridge, Massachusetts: Harvard University Press, 2001.

Index

100 Huntley Street, 56
Allan, Rev. David, 20
Apostolic Church in Canada, 18
Argue, A. H. (Andrew Harvey), 2, 3, 13
Argue, Elwin (evangelist), 3, 14, 15, 16, 76, 77
Argue, Zelma (evangelist), 3, 13, 14, 89
Atter, Gordon, 10, 12, 94
Azusa Street Revival, 2, 63, 93, 100
Barnett, Caroline, 60
Bell, Charles, 21
Bethel Manor, 42
Bethel Pentecostal Church, i, iii, iv, v, vii, viii, ix, x, xi, 1, 17, 19, 30, 31, 32, 33, 34, 35, 36, 37, 39, 40, 41, 43, 44, 45, 46, 47, 50, 54, 55, 56, 57, 58, 59, 60, 61, 62, 65, 79, 80, 81, 89, 95, 96, 97, 98, 99, 100
Blair, J. H. (J. Harold), 27, 31, 35, 96
Bombay, Ken, 35, 52
Bothwell, Ontario, 13, 16, 95
Bradbury, Ray, 57, 58
Bradley, Mike (mayor), 55
Braeside Pentecostal Camp, ix, 21, 22, 23, 24, 63, 96, 100
Bright's Grove, 46, 47, 98

Brownsville Revival (Pensacola, Florida), 45, 54, 58
Buffum, Judy, 45
Buntain, Huldah, 57, 59, 60
Buntain, Mark, 16, 57
Burden, Frank, 27, 29
Carroll, Paul, 41
Carroll, Rev. George, 40, 41, 55, 95, 97, 98
Carruthers, Mary (née Elliot), 56
Celaire, Rich and Lavinia, 57
Cooley, Lindell, 58, 59
Corbett, Phillip, 57
Corunna, Ontario, 43
Courtright Pentecostal Church (Courtright, Ontario), 42
Curran and Herridge Contractors (Sarnia, Ontario), 30
Curran, Sue, 52
Davy, Mark (evangelist), 52, 57
Dickson, Ed, 57, 59
Dunne, Dorothy (organist), 36, 37, 79, 89, 97
Dunnville, Ontario, 26, 33, 96
Eastern Pentecostal Bible College. *See* Master's College and Seminary
Fitch, Rev. W., 30

Forrest, Charles, 16
Fourfold Gospel, 1, 11, 22, 45, 60
Free Methodist, 8, 19, 20, 21, 73
Froese, Allen, 52, 53, 89
Fulham, Jerry, 40, 41
Full Gospel. *See* Fourfold Gospel
Full Gospel Mission, 12, 30
Full Gospel Tabernacle, 14, 17, 77, 95
Gaetz, Edith, 10
Galati, Dominic, Jr. (evangelist), 57
Galessiere, Gianpaolo and Alicia, 48
Gibb, Cayden, 56
Gibb, Kim, 47, 48, 56
Gibb, Margaret, 48
Gibb, Rev. Robert, 48
Gibb, Rev. Tim, viii, x, 47, 48, 49, 50, 51, 52, 57, 60, 61, 81, 99, 100
Gibb, Tricia, 48, 56, 57
Gibson, William and Margaret, 20
Gingrich, Ab, 40, 55
Gingrich, Joyce (née Thompson), 30, 36
Gonyon, Eric, 60
Goodwin, Joanne, 56
Grasseschi, Faytene (née Kryskow), 52
Griffin, Mark, 56
Guerette, Chris, 55
Hammond, James, 26, 33, 96, 98
Harris, Harry C. (evangelist), 10
Hawkins, Steve, 56
Heaven's Gates and Hell's Flames, 57
Hebden, Ellen and James, 2, 3, 4, 5, 68, 74, 75, 91, 92, 94
Helps, Rev. Dan, 46

Hessler, David, 57
Hick, Grant, 41
Holmes, Greg, 51
Holy Spirit, xi, 1, 2, 3, 4, 5, 6, 7, 8, 9, 11, 12, 17, 21, 22, 34, 36, 45, 51, 54, 56, 61, 64, 67, 68, 69, 70, 71, 72, 73, 74, 91, 92, 93, 97
Howard-Browne, Rodney, 60
India, 4, 6, 7, 57, 60, 72, 74, 75, 76
Johnston, Barbara, v, x, 4, 5, 6, 7, 8, 60, 72, 92
Johnston, John, 4, 72
Jolley, Frank, 10, 30, 31, 32, 33, 93
Kasey, Reva (evangelist), 50, 52
Kemsley, Etta, 21
Kerychuk, Mike, 52, 56
Kilpatrick, Rev. John, 45, 56
King's Kids Nursery School, 41
Lakeshore Community Church (Bright's Grove, Ontario), 46, 47
Lapier, Kim, 56
Leghorn, Jessie, 21
Liira, Rev. Bert, 43, 44, 45
Liira, Shirley, 43
Livengood, Michael (evangelist), 45, 57
London, Ontario, 10, 20
Lucas County, Ohio, 20
Mainse, David, 56
Manafo, Joe, 46
Mann, Don, 57, 58
Marrow, Lydia (née Stanley), 58, 59
Martin, Dr. Larry (evangelist), 56
Master's College and Seminary, 41, 42, 43, 94, 98
Master's Pentecostal Seminary, x
McAlister, R. E. (Robert Edward), 2, 10, 16

McAlister, Walter, 10
McPherson, Aimee Semple, 64
Moore, Steve, 43
Morris, Nathan (evangelist), 56, 58, 59
Morrow, Rev. William, 41, 42, 43, 98
Mukti Mission, 6, 76, 92
Nelson, Rev. C., 32, 93, 96
Nettleship, Rev. Gary, 45, 46, 47, 57
Norcross, Rev. Robert, Sr., 33, 34, 35, 36, 37, 38
Norton, Albert and Mary, 6
Norton, John, 6, 7, 72, 92
Oosthuyzen, Steve (evangelist), 45
Ouellette, Jordan, 56
Ozman, Agnes, 8, 9, 92
Painter, Jan, 60
Parham, Charles, 8, 9, 63, 92, 93
Paris, Ontario, 21, 23
Parkway Pentecostal Church (Corunna, Ontario), 43
Parry Sound, Ontario, 10, 33, 89, 94, 98
Patrick, Rev. Keith and Patricia, 54
Paulsen, Les and Lois, 42, 44
Pentecostal Assemblies of Canada, ix, 9, 10, 12, 22, 26, 27, 29, 30, 31, 39, 43, 48, 57, 93, 94, 97, 98, 99, 100; Western Ontario District, iii, 22, 27, 31, 43
Polymer Corporation (Sarnia, Ontario), 28
Powell, Ken, 40, 42
Powers, Max, 17
Quebec, 11, 41, 48
Ramabai, Pandita, 6, 76
Raycroft, Randy, 45

Renfro, Dr. Tom and Sid, 50
Riblet, Edna, v, 1, 19, 20, 21, 22, 23, 25, 26, 27, 28, 29, 33, 60, 61, 63, 78, 96, 98
Riblet, John, 20
Richardson, Tom, 16, 39, 40
Robertson, Rev. Carey, 45
Roth, Sid, 52
Routley, A. O. (Almond Obadiah), 28, 34, 37
Routley, Charlie, 34, 42, 44, 61
Routley, Rev. Jim, 37
Rutledge, Glen, 56
Rutledge, Rev. David, 43
Salford, Ontario, 64
Salvation Army, 10, 21
Sarnia Collegiate Institute and Technical School (SCITS), 55
Sarnia Revival, v, 49, 50, 51, 52, 53, 99
Sarnia, Ontario, i, iii, iv, v, vii, viii, x, xi, 12, 1, 3, 4, 5, 6, 7, 8, 9, 10, 11, 12, 13, 14, 15, 16, 19, 20, 21, 22, 26, 28, 30, 32, 33, 36, 39, 40, 42, 43, 45, 46, 47, 49, 50, 53, 54, 60, 61, 62, 63, 68, 72, 75, 76, 77, 78, 89, 92, 93, 94, 95, 96, 97, 98, 99, 100; Essex Street, v, 1, 30, 34, 36, 38, 39, 40, 41, 80, 97; Lakeview Cemetery, 7, 30; Lincoln Park, 26; Lochiel Street, 9, 17; London Line, iv, v, 1, 39, 44, 80, 97; Mitton Street, 12, 17; North Front Street, 10, 11; Oxford Street, 19, 26; Victoria Street North, 9; White Street, v, 1, 19, 20, 21, 26, 27, 28, 29, 30, 61
Scarrella, Tom (evangelist), 51, 52

Schoch, Rev. Paul, 45

Shuttlesworth, Ted (evangelist), 50, 57, 60

Sombra Township, Ontario, 20

Spinks, Sue, 47

St. Catharines, Ontario, 10

Stephan, A. E. (Adeline Elizabeth), 10, 11, 12, 13, 17, 19, 26, 30, 78, 94, 97

Stewart, John and Beverlie, 44, 45

Stewart, Tracy, 60

Stratton, Lyndon, 56

Swanson, Rev. James, 12

Taff, Russ, 60

Taran, Lena, 58

Terminus, Ontario, 20

The Pentecostal Testimony, x, 9, 10, 11, 12, 14, 22, 27, 31, 78, 89, 93, 94, 95, 96, 97

The Sarnia Canadian Observer, 13, 14, 15, 16, 35, 36, 40, 76, 78, 79, 81, 89, 93, 94, 95, 98, 99

Toby, Rev. Troy, 46

Tongues, 3, 69, 71, 72, 92

Toronto, Ontario, v, 2, 3, 5, 6, 33, 68, 73, 74, 76, 91, 92, 96, 97

Tosh, Harry, 34, 36, 98

Tubby, C. S. (evangelist), 32

Tweedie, Dr. John, 57

Ukraine, 58

Vegh, Moses, 45

Wallaceburg, Ontario, 28

Warren, Brian, 50, 52

Wells, Rev. David, 57

White Street Mission, v, 19, 20, 21, 26, 27, 28, 29, 30

Wilkinson, John (evangelist), 57

Williams, Arthur and Letitia, 16

Williams, Dr. Randall, 16

Williams, Rev. Earl, 16, 30

Wilson, S. H. (Samuel), 13, 16, 95

Windsor, Ontario, 12, 30, 41

Winnipeg, 2, 3, 10, 13, 14, 16, 77, 91, 94

Winter, Bob (evangelist), 45

Worship, xi, 1, 32, 42, 47, 50, 51, 52, 58, 59

Zion Bible College, 47

Corrigenda
(inserted 2021)

Page 7

Barbara A. Johnston is stated incorrectly to have been "**buried in**" the Johnston family plot at Lakeview Cemetery in Sarnia. In fact, she was "**buried in India, and a memorial stone was placed on**" the Johnston family plot at Lakeview Cemetery in Sarnia.

Page 84

The following names should have been included:

BETHEL PENTECOSTAL CHURCH:
OTHER PASTORAL STAFF

1970's
Angus & Rose Nicholson (Music)
Newell & Elsie Wendt (Seniors)

Page 87

The following name should have been included:

ELDER BOARD OF DIRECTORS

2006-2016
Ken Tosh (2015)

Updates

The following updates may be noted (2021).

ADDITIONS: OTHER PASTORAL STAFF

2010's

Jennifer Winklmeier (Children's Ministries)
Brock & Kirsten Wright (Youth & Junior High)

2020's

Neil & Bethanie Armstrong (Outreach & Discipleship)
Hannah Chamas (Youth & Junior High)
Tricia Gibb (Executive Pastor)
Dale & Carolyn Ruttan (Children's Ministries & Junior High)
Kerby & Mary Stivene (Youth & Young Adults)
Jennifer Winklmeier (Children's Ministries)

ADDITIONS: ELDER BOARD OF DIRECTORS
2006-2021

Keiryn Ajayiobe (2020) Rob Taylor (2019)
Jenson Charles (2020) Colin Winklmeier (2021)
Laureen Elliott (2020)

AVERAGE SUNDAY ATTENDANCE

Year	S.S.	AM	PM
2016	N/A	426	116
2017	N/A	418	107
2018	N/A	419	104
2019	N/A	391	93
2020*	N/A	287	0

2020 attendance statistics were difficult to track because of periods of online-only services, drive-in services, and an imposed in-person limit of 30% seating capacity (for services at 9:15 AM and 11 AM each Sunday) during the COVID-19 pandemic. Online attendance was included in the average calculation in 2020 because of online-only services and imposed limits on in-person gatherings. This was tracked by the number of devices connected, although in most cases there would have been more than one viewer per device.

* 9 7 8 0 9 9 5 3 2 9 9 0 4 *